The Great Revival Mandate

Mantled For

The Shaking of the Nations

NORMAN MOREA TRENT SABADI

Author of Chosen to Carry the Glory – Carry the Fire of Jesus

Norman Morea Trent Sabadi

AUTHOR OF
Chosen to Carry The Glory – Carry the Fire of Jesus

The Great Revival Mandate

MANTLED

For the shaking of the nations

> The Lord God will shake the nations and fill His House with His Glory

For you,

- -

May the Glory of the Word rest mightily upon you!

© Norman Morea Trent Sabadi 2025

All rights reserved. This book is protected by the copyright laws of Australia. This book may not be transmitted, copied or reprinted in any form for commercial gain or profit, without the prior written permission of the publisher or author. Permission will be granted upon request. The use of short quotations or occasional page copying for personal or group study, for sermons, and social media posts, for audio and video content, is permitted and encouraged, with acknowledgements.

Unless otherwise identified, scriptural quotations are taken from the Holy Bible (The King James Version).

Cover Design by Norman Sabadi Media Productions 2025

ISBN (Paperback Standard B&W):   978-0-9756110-5-0
ISBN (Paperback Premium Colour):   978-0-9756110-9-8
ISBN (Hardcover B&W):   978-0-9756110-6-7
ISBN (Hardcover Premium Colour):   978-1-7642930-0-6
ISBN (Ebook - pdf):   978-0-9756110-7-4
ISBN (Ebook - Kindle):   978-0-9756110-8-1

For Worldwide Distribution

Norman Sabadi Publishing
Gracemere, QLD 4702, Australia

NOTES FOR THIS BOOK

Note 1: (The English language has limitations like any other language) For the sake of the reader: to keep the flow of thought and maintain simplicity, 'man' also includes 'woman' and 'he' includes 'she' WHERE APPLICABLE—the inclusive thought applies. This is to emphasise that the "Holy Calling" of God is to both man and woman, boy and girl. For example: a female reader is encouraged to see herself as "Chosen" where I have just said, "God will use 'him' for His Glory"—replace 'him' with 'her.'

Note 2: You find this also in certain parts of the scriptures, like *John 1:12*, which mentions 'sons' only (but does not exclude daughters—ancient language was inclusive of both genders where it was expressed, within context). Other parts of scripture include 'daughters.' For example, *Acts 2:17, which* includes 'sons and daughters.' Therefore, where *contextually applicable,* 'sons' also includes 'daughters;' and 'fathers' and 'leaders' include 'mothers.'

Note 3: A great portion of the leaders of the Church today are mainly pastors. So, I may occasionally use the term 'pastors' to refer to *leaders,* but I am not leaving out the apostles, prophets, teachers and evangelists. I may also interchangeably (and occasionally) use the words 'ministers,' 'fathers,' 'leaders,' 'elders,' or 'clergy' to refer to the leaders—the shepherds of the flock.

Note 4: Certain words in this book have the first letter in uppercase referring to "God" and emphasis towards the "Revival" theme of this book, where applicable. This occurs right through the book. This is to express reverence and honour to God (This list of words and other related words):
- Him, He, His, You, Your, Yours, Me, My
- His Wings,
- Holy One, Jesus Christ, Lord, God

- Glory, Power, Fire, Presence, Word, Abiding Word, Word of Glory,
- New Day, Dawn of a New Day, Awakening, His Promised Blessing, The Great Revival Awakening, The Great Outpouring, The Promise, The Glory Day, Power from on High, Baptism of Fire, Move of God, His Movement
- Revival, Revival Fire, Revival Anointing, Mantle,
- Church, House, His House,
- Heaven's Cause, Commission, Mandate,
- Holy Spirit, Holy Ghost, Comforter, Counsellor
- Revivalist, Burning One, Sent One, Fire Carrier, Glory Carrier,
- His Army, Gideon Army,
- Truth, The Light, Life
- Burning Bush, Upper Room,
- Divine, Divine Passion, His Abundance, His Work, Plan and Purpose of Heaven
- The Place Where He Speaks.
- Grace, Truth, Peace, and Power

Note 5: My writing style is mainly an expository-exegesis, and at times expositional. I write with a strong prophetic edge and apostolic fervour, being led by the Holy Spirit. The reader is encouraged to pursue the deepness of the Word from the start of the book to the final words of the book.

God invites you to be a part of the most phenomenal and historic event of all time—the Great Revival Awakening. For at the appointed time, the Glory of God shall descend upon us, and fill His House with glad tidings.

Dedication

To You, Lord Jesus, with all of my heart.

Acknowledgements

Jesus, my Lord and Savour: I love You more than anything. I thank You for Your abundant Grace poured so generously upon my life. How I love Your Presence and the Glory of Your Word.

My beloved wife, Olivia, and children, Ethan and Jazmina: You are God's precious gift to me. Thank you for standing unwaveringly by my side through this God-assignment. May the *Day of the Lord's Great Revival Awakening* rest mightily upon You.

My sincere thanks to Dr. Miriam Lili: Your careful eye, patience, and thoughtful input have been a Divine blessing in carrying this book triumphantly to completion.

To the beloved family of The Place Where He Speaks: Words cannot contain the immense joy of sharing this glorious, Holy Ghost Truths with you! We have journeyed together—through gentle brooks, across the deep valleys and upon the radiant mountaintops. Together, we have seen God's Fire burn and His Glory manifest in wondrous ways. What an extraordinary hour we are in. From my heart to yours, you are all remarkable, anointed and chosen ministers of God. May the glorious Fire of His Revival Anointing rest mightily upon you, for the shaking of the nations.

To the faithful and steadfast saints: You have pursued the Presence of the Lord with unwavering earnestness and pure sincerity, yielding your hearts fully to the Holy Ghost. Now, take courage! Lift up your heads, and behold—*the Dawn of the New Day of His Glory* is about to break upon us, overflowing with exceeding abundance. Rejoice, for *the Day of the Great Awakening is near—the Zeal of the Lord shall perform it.*

Contents

Contents

PREFACE	19

Why I Wrote this Book

Part 1 - Genesis of the Glory Carrier—"And God Said..."

CHAPTER 1	29

Genesis of the Glory Carrier… "And God Said"

Part 2 - Mantled for the Great Revival Mandate: the Call & Commission

CHAPTER 2	43

The Great Revival Mandate

CHAPTER 3	53

The Mighty Release of Mantles

Part 3 - The Preparatory Moves & Mentorship for the Move

CHAPTER 4	65

Mentorship: The Prerequisite for the Move of God

CHAPTER 5	75

The Preliminary Revival Fires Are Already Here

Part 4 - The Birth of the Great Move (Prophetic Foundations)

CHAPTER 6	83

The Ordained Birth of the Great Awakening is at Hand

CHAPTER 7	91

PROPHECY: the Great Move of God Will Start in Papua New Guinea

Part 5 - God's Chosen Leader—The Revivalist

CHAPTER 8	109

Sheep With No Shepherd

Contents

CHAPTER 9 — 115
Leader of the Great Revival

CHAPTER 10 — 123
Marked With Fire

Part 6 - The Elijah Mantle: Preparing the Way Again

CHAPTER 11 — 135
The Spirit & Power of Elijah—the Revivalist

CHAPTER 12 — 145
The Prophetic Continuation of the Revival Theme

CHAPTER 13 — 155
The Spirit & Power of Elijah in John the Baptist

CHAPTER 14 — 163
'Yohannan'

CHAPTER 15 — 171
The Spirit & Power of Elijah in the Church

Part 7 - Fathering the Move of God

CHAPTER 16 — 185
Lukewarmness, Fatherlessness Crisis, & the Turning of Hearts

CHAPTER 17 — 199
Spirit-led Fathers Raise Spirit-led Sons

Part 8 - Reclaiming the Fire of the Upper Room

CHAPTER 18 — 215
Leaders of Babel vs. Leaders of the Upper Room

Part 9 - The Posture that Attracts, Hosts, & Releases the Glory

CHAPTER 19 — 225
The Spirit of the Lord Shall Raise A Standard

CHAPTER 20 — 237
The Uncut Stone

Contents

Part 10 - The Credo & Passion of the Revivalist

CHAPTER 21 — 249
The Praying Preacher

CHAPTER 22 — 261
Preparation & Depth of the Praying Preacher

Part 11 - The Word of Glory & The Mantled Vessel

CHAPTER 23 — 273
Revival Architecture

Part 12 - The Trumpet Sounds—It's Time for Revival!

CHAPTER 24 — 285
The Trumpet Sounds — It's Time for Revival!

About the Author — 294

Opening Prayer

We bow down before Your Throne of Grace and worship You, Lord, for You are our God. We come before you with the posture that brings Your Glory. We are ready, Lord—to receive the fullness of Your Grace.

Oh, Holy One (*Ha'kadosh*), God of the Great Revival Fire. Descend and rest upon us with the Glory of Your Word. Holy Spirit, we ask that You have Your Way in us. For we have chosen to behold the Glory of Your Presence and to abide under the Shadow of Your Wings.

Arise, oh God, to Your rest. Come to us with the Power and magnificence of Your Glory. Let the Wind of Your Spirit blow upon our hearts, and may we respond with willing obedience. May we know that it is You at work in our midst. For we have come to behold the fullness of Your Glory.

Prepare us, oh Holy One. Prepare us to receive Your glorious Revival Fire. The break of Dawn is near, oh Lord… Descend upon us *Adonai—Yahweh*, and glorify the House of Your Glory.

(*Qadosh Adonai, ki hu Qadosh*—holy is the Lord our God) Hallelujah!

In *Yeshua's Name*…

Amen!

There is a Place by Him, full of Grace and tender Mercies. There, in His Presence, we are complete as we behold the fullness of His Glory.

PREFACE

Why I Wrote this Book

There is a Place by Me.

I have had wonderful times in the Holy Ghost. I have experienced the fullness of the Power of God, and I can tell you there is nothing like it. I can't think of a better place or experience that can measure up to the Power of His Glory. I have been so taken by the Lord that the more I pursue God, the more I have become *broken and recklessly abandoned for His Glory*. I prefer to be this way before my Lord. For my delight is *His Desire* and *His Delight* is my desire (Psalms 37:4). It's a *First Love* experience—I can't explain in words, but when you have chosen Him, and He has chosen you—that is something special.

I have beheld and been captivated by the magnificence of His Glory. And I have walked in *the Power of His Presence,* and whenever I knew He was there, it felt to me like the Great Shepherd leading me beside the still waters (Psalms 23). In those holy moments, when His Power rests on my being, I then feel like a sheep being led by the Shepherd-King, and I want nothing else; I need nothing else but Him. My one desire is for Jesus to be revealed through me. I must decrease, so that He can increase and be fully manifested to the world.

That being said, I know in my heart that the Holy Spirit wanted me to write this for you, and I have obeyed Him... This is for you, His precious ones. For you are *the Apple of His Eye*.

I begin my initial thoughts by looking back to that wonderful night of my *Fire-Baptism* (Friday night, 27th August 1999),[1] which came to me, as a *"Suddenly,"* when the Holy Spirit blew like a *Wind and His weighty Mantle* rested upon my being. I can best describe the encounter as Heaven touching Earth (Acts 2:1–4). The memory is still so vivid—I was completely *immersed in His fiery Anointing and overflowing with His Power.* It felt like I had entered a new realm in Christ Jesus, with a real and deep knowing of the Power of God. A *Revival Anointing* rested on me and gave me access to a dimension of God so tangible and beyond words. Before that, I never knew that such a *place* in God was real. But here I was, *drenched with holy Fire,* and it was amazing.

I believe these wonderful encounters and experiences are available to every believer today. The fullness of God wants to be with man, and His Glory desires to be in our midst. This remains the Holy Spirit's endeavour for us (Exodus 29:43–46).

On this note, I want to thank you for picking up this Glory Carriers—Revival Fire book, and taking the time to read what I believe is a NOW WORD for the Church.

I testify *by the Spirit of Prophecy* that an unprecedented, tangible outpouring of the Holy Ghost is about to descend upon the Earth in a mighty way. And I have been *mantled and mandated* by the Holy Spirit to write about this *Glory Event.* I do not take this assignment lightly, because I know that abundant Grace has been poured upon me to speak about this monumental encounter. For "A man can receive nothing unless it be given him *from Heaven* (John 3:27, Ephesians 4:7)."

...*The Great Revival (Awakening) Fire*—that's what it's called. It goes by other names, also:
- The Greatest Outpouring of the Holy Spirit
- The Greatest Awakening
- The Great Tide of His Glory
- The Mighty Wind of the Spirit
- The Light of the Knowledge of the Glory
- The Glory of the Lord that shall shake the Nations
- The Glory of the latter House
- The (Knowledge of the) Glory of the Lord

Over the years, the Holy Spirit has deepened my understanding and revelation of this prodigious *Glory Encounter*. Especially in recent years, the Lord has begun to speak expressly and in more detail about this forthcoming *Glory Event*.

Like Isaiah, I, too, have been undone before the Lord of Glory (Isaiah 6:1–8). And my heart beats with excitement for *the Glory-Day* that is fast approaching. It will be the most beautiful, the most historical, the most momentous, unimaginable, nation-shaking experience ever. It will be a *Day of days, and Season of seasons*, preparing the hearts of many for the coming King—Christ Jesus, the Lord of Glory.

So, I write this with *a one accord spirit and attitude.* The same kind of one accord that *drew the Glory* to the Upper Room in Jerusalem and turned heads and hearts in its direction (Acts 2:1–17). I join in agreement with *Heaven's Cause* for this most notable *Commission* given to us, earthen vessels.

2 Corinthians 4:5–7

For we preach not ourselves, but Christ Jesus the Lord; and ourselves your servants for Jesus' sake. For God, who commanded *the Light* to shine out of darkness, hath shined in our hearts, to give the Light

PREFACE — *Why I wrote This Book*

of *the Knowledge of the Glory of God* in the Face of Jesus Christ. But we have *this treasure* in earthen vessels, that the excellency of the Power may be of God, and not of us.

I have written this book for you, not as a perfect man, but as a broken man, transformed by unbiased, selfless *Grace*. I write as one soaked by *His Revival Anointing*. Like Moses, I also have responded to *the Call* to ascend to that place of places—*the Place of the cleft of the Rock*. And like Elijah, who heard the "sound of rain," I can also hear *the Sound of Revival* intensifying as He draws near. The Revival Trumpet resounds, and the Spirit of Prophecy shall reach His crescendo. For *the Light of Dawn* shall break forth upon us at the appointed time.

I considered this *privilege to see and hear as a holy burden from the Spirit*, burning in me like Fire that cannot be quenched. These *Oracles of God must be delivered* to the Body of Christ. As God's messenger, I know that I am accountable to Him. *This is my appointed burden that I must carry for His Cause*. And the Fire of the Word burns... I can't relent—I must speak (Jeremiah 20:9). I must blow *the Trumpet of Revival*. Why then should I hide what the Lord is doing? Even if I wanted to, the Fire within me won't be silent, and He will compel me to speak (Jeremiah 20:9, 2 Corinthians 3:12).

This is my gaze right now: A mighty *Mantle to carry the Glory* is about to descend upon the Church, and His Glory shall be seen in her. Hallelujah! And when His Glory is poured upon us, the Great Shepherd shall come and lead us; He shall lead us into *the Waters of His Revival* gushing forth so splendidly for us. I believe that it is also because we have looked to that glorious Day with hope, and with great expectation in our hearts. Because God wants us to search for Him with all our heart—it's a prerequisite of the Revival Fire (Jeremiah 29:10–13, Isaiah 55:5–7).

Why I wrote This Book **PREFACE**

Can you hear the *Voice of the Spirit?* He says, "Come to the Table of the King of Glory. Come, oh precious ones, to the feast that has been prepared for you. For the Cup of His Great Awakening is overflowing there." Assuredly, the Lord shall do a good and glorious work in us—for He shall write *His Word, His Ways, His Thoughts, and His Desires* upon our hearts by His Holy Spirit (Ezekiel 36:25–27, Jeremiah 31:33-34, Ephesians 3:20, 2 Corinthians 3:3–4). The perils and tribulations of this time should not discourage or hinder you from pursuing Him.

Oh, that you would gaze into His lovely Presence. For the Spirit beckons you with heartfelt Grace to come and partake—*He wants you to be prepared to receive His Glory.* The Lord Jesus wants this for you more than you can ever imagine. *God is pursuing You—Glory wants to rest upon you.* Friends, the gentle, powerful Voice of Jesus is speaking to you in this hour, saying, "Let not your heart be troubled: you believe in God, believe also in Me… *I go to prepare a Place for you* (John 14:1–3)…" And He has prepared not just Heaven for us, but also a *place of encounter,* which is soon ready to descend upon us with glad tidings. Hallelujah! For the Father's Heart will be fully manifested to us on the Day of His Glory Outpouring. I speak to you, *Burning Ones.* You are God's *Gideon Army.* The atmosphere is turning in our favour because the time of His mandated Revival is upon us. *Gouloka!*[2] —We shall see the breaking of First Light—the Dawn of the New Day of the Holy Ghost.

Finally, I want to proclaim a word of blessing over you. May you receive the fullness of His Peace and Power! And may the Glory of His Revival Fire rest mightily upon you as you turn your hearts to Jesus and respond to *His Prophetic Trumpet* to be a part of *His Army of Glory Carriers.*

PREFACE — *Why I wrote This Book*

May the Day of the Great Awakening Be Yours!

"Servant of the place of the cleft of the Rock—The Place Where He Speaks."

Norman Morea Trent Sabadi

Prayer:

Oh Comforter and Counsellor, breathe upon the pages of this book with Power and life. Let these Words carry Your intent and cause Your people to catch the Great Revival Fire. For Revival comes only from You and You alone. Oh Lord God of Glory, may this book bring glory to Your Name. We pray earnestly for Your will to be done—be it unto us, according to Your Word! In Yeshua's Name, Amen.

ENDNOTE:

1. Sabadi, N.M.T, 2023. Chapter 2 Baptised With the Holy Ghost & Fire, *Chosen to Carry the Glory—Carry the Fire of Jesus*, Norman Sabadi Publishing, Rockhampton, Queensland, Australia, pp.31-49).

2. Sabadi, N.M.T, 2023. "Gouloka - meaning, the dawn of a new day, or at the break of dawn." Language: Eastern Highlands Province, Papua New Guinea, Chapter 1, Where It All Began, *Chosen to Carry the Glory—Carry the Fire of Jesus*, Norman Sabadi Publishing, Rockhampton, Queensland, Australia, p.22).

Why I wrote This Book   PREFACE

Part 1 – Genesis of the Glory Carrier—"And God Said..."

And God said, "Let us make man in Our Image and after Our Likeness…"

—*Genesis 1:27*

CHAPTER 1

Genesis of the Glory Carrier... "And God Said"

And the LORD God formed man of the dust of the ground, and breathed into his nostrils the Breath of Life; and man became a living soul.

Genesis 2:7

From the very beginning, God wanted fellowship, and He wanted to share the fullness of Himself. Then He decided it was *time to fulfil that thought*. God was going to create a being *just like Himself*. At that time, the Earth was without form and void (Genesis 1:1), and there was no light as yet—just pitch darkness. The Spirit began to *hover over the waters*. It was not a random thing...No, God was postured to carry out His Plan—a plan not only to create all things, but to create something most precious and wonderful.

Three thoughts come to mind as to why the Spirit was *hovering over the waters*:

- It was to prepare *the Way* for *His Word*,

- The Spirit of God was *ready to act upon the Word—released* at the *appointed Time.*
- And then *He Spoke...*

"Then God said...

Everything that was destined to become reality *depended on this one thing—He Spoke His Word...* What an amazing opening statement! Everything came *obediently* into existence in response to the *sound of His Voice,* each bearing its own purpose and place, and all because *God said, or God spoke.*

Hebrews 11:3
Through faith we understand that the worlds were framed by *the Word of God,* so that things which are seen were not made of things which do appear.

The Glory of the Spoken Word

The key thought—or the centre of our attention here—is *The Glory of the Spoken Word.* This is the foundation and essence of the Revival Theme—the Mandate, and *the Mantle* to carry it.

The apostle John caught the fullness of this revelation as he began writing the opening lines of his account of the Gospel story... "*In the beginning was the Word, and the Word was with (or next to) God, and the Word was God. The Same* was in the beginning with God. All things were made by Him; and without Him was not any thing made that was made. *In Him was Life; and the Life was the Light of men.* And the Light shineth in darkness; and the darkness comprehended it not (John 1:1-5)." John was giving us insight into that first and foremost opening statement—when God said.

The Glory-Mantle Upon Man —the Glory Blueprint Begins

In Genesis, the Glory of the Word was to become *flesh in man (Adam). But first, an earthen vessel (a human) was formed by the Hand of God and made ready to receive God's first Breath (A Glory-filled Breath) — with Power, Life, Personality, Mind, Authority, Identity, and Language.* The Word wasn't only just the Life and Light of man, but the Life and Light *dwelling in man.* The Glory that flowed from Adam was now like a brightly lit city on a hill, that cannot be hidden (Matthew 5:14). The first man shone bright, and it was a marvellous thing to behold. In fact, God looked at His beautiful masterpiece and He said it was "very good" (Genesis 1:31).

You can now understand a little bit more about how God must have felt when man's light became dim and completely non-existent on the day he disobeyed God. But the Lord still loved mankind (Exodus 34:5–7). And He continued to *speak*—so much that *He spoke* again through the prophet Isaiah, saying, "Arise and shine for your Light has come, and the Glory of the Lord is risen upon you...The Lord shall rise upon you, and His Glory shall be *seen upon you* (Isaiah 60:1–2)." God would not let go of His original intent for us *as Glory Carriers*, and He never will. The unchanging God still looks from Heaven, and His eyes are still upon the hearts of mankind, looking for one defining hallmark—a man that *trembles at His Word* (Isaiah 61:1–2). Hallelujah! This *recurring motif* is seen throughout the scriptures, from Genesis to Revelation. God's Truth *never changes. He (Jesus Christ)* is *the same* yesterday, today, and forever (Hebrews 13:8). Therefore, we can trust the reliability of His infallible Truth—in fact, He is Truth (Numbers 23:19, John 14:6).

John 17:14–17
I (Jesus) have given them Thy Word…Sanctify them through Thy Truth: Thy Word is Truth.

From the very beginning, mankind's design was that we would never be without *His Word*. God's Word was not just meant to be our life-source; His Word was to *remain in us and abide in our beings. Man was to be clothed with the Glory of the Word*—in the fullness of the resemblance of his Creator and *Father*. Our design took on more than just made from the dust (*Adama*)[3] of the earth. *The Ruach (Spirit)—Wind, Breath, Life, Personality, Mind and Glory of God was put into man (Adam)* (Genesis 2:7). Thus, God's Word in man began with a Breath and became *Glory-substance in him*.

Man was mantled to be more than just a creature. Adam never considered for a moment that he was naked, because he was completely robed with the Mantle of the Glory, which rested weightily and majestically upon his being (Genesis 2:25). Adam was beautifully formed and richly clothed. His splendour was more than anything King Solomon, or any other royal, could ever achieve (Matthew 6:29). That Mantle started to really show when God gave Adam *the right and blessing* of naming all the animals (Genesis 2:19).

Additional thought:
God is also man's Father. Adam learned how to live and walk in his identity as a Glory Carrier by communing with his Father. God was man's first Mentor, Leader and Guide. That's why Jesus came to teach us that God is our Father, not in a religious way, but a relational way. Jesus also said it was expedient that He completed His part of the Glory Mandate and returned to the Father (Isaiah 55:10–13), promising that He would send the Spirit (John 16:7). Then, the Glory of the

Word was once again released to clothe man as our Comforter-Counsellor: to Mentor, Lead and Guide the Church. The Glory-mantled life began in the first Adam when God said... And now, the pathway to fulfilment of its restoration is meant to be fully realised and received by the Church. (This was made possible in Christ Jesus, the second Adam).

Redeemed Glory Carriers

At the time when man was banished from the Garden of Eden, he had lost his way altogether and was lost in iniquity and disobedience. *When man lost his way, he also lost his identity.* He was immediately aware that he had lost his Glory-Mantle and that the world was a cold place (spiritually). But a part of Adam still longed for fellowship with God. It seems that even then, the deep within man was calling out to *the Deep of the Glory* that he so recently walked in.

Confronted by this new reality—a sin-affected world—Adam (and his wife Eve) would likely have thought to themselves, *"Will God, their Father, ever find it in His heart to receive them again?"* Despite man's fall, God still wanted to *redeem him*. For God so loved...man. A Redemptive Plan was already in motion *in the Father's Heart*.

Why is all this important for us to note? Because, for us to understand the necessity and importance of *the coming Glory,* we must first understand the *original design* of the Glory in us, and on us. From God's perspective, our *Genesis* is the basis and reason for our Redemption. Therefore, the work of Revival is *the pathway* back to *who we were* designed to be... **Glory Carriers.**

We can see why the apostle John later said, "Beloved, now are we *the sons of God*, and it doth not yet appear what we shall be: but we know that, *when He shall appear, we shall be like Him; for we shall see Him (The Word) as He is* (1 John 3:2)."

The *knowing and fullness* of our identity (in Him) remains in His Words. That's why Jesus told Satan, "Man shall not live by bread alone, but by *every Word that proceeds out from the Mouth of God (Matthew 4:4)."*

The framework and infilling of the *House of God—which is the Church*—are laid upon the foundation of our *Genesis*, when God spoke His *Word of Glory* into us. That is why the Word is our foundation, and our *Cornerstone* (Psalms 118:22–23, Acts 4:11-12, Zechariah 3:9, Zechariah 4). THE WORD that spoke man into existence and filled him with God's Glory is the same glorious Word that shall be *spoken into us* to reinstate our place as Glory Carriers—chosen by God.

Three key thoughts stand out explicitly from this:

- **Our Genesis:** *The Foundation*—designed to carry the Glory.
- **Our Salvation and Redemption:** *The Framework of the House*—"built upon the foundation of the apostles and prophets with Jesus Christ Himself as the chief Cornerstone; in whom all the building fitly framed together groweth unto a Holy Temple in the Lord: in whom ye also are *built together for an habitation of God through the Spirit* (Ephesians 2:20–22)"
- **Our Sanctification and Glorification:** *The Glory of the Word, will once again speak* with Grace and Truth—upon us, and into us—to abide with us and be in our midst (Romans 8:16-18).

2 Corinthians 4:6–7

For God, who commanded the Light to shine out of darkness, hath shined in our hearts, to give the Light of the Knowledge of the Glory of God in the Face of Jesus Christ. **But we have this Treasure in earthen vessels,** that the excellency of the Power may be of God, and not of us.

God Thought—God Spoke—God Wrote

Now, when God said… He *thought it first*, and then it was also *written*. God documented what He said to His prophets.

"He thought—He spoke—He wrote.

That is why Jesus said, "It is written." Likewise, the coming Glory is not only going to be a—*God said*, but also a—*God wrote in us* (Jeremiah 31:33). The decree of the King of kings has been written, that His Glory shall abide with man. This *key thought* is also modelled in Jesus, as the example and pioneer of *the Redeemed-Glory-Carrier* (Ezekiel 11:19, Ezekiel 36:26).

Psalms 40:7–8
Then said I, Lo, I come: in the volume of the book **it is written of me,** I delight to do thy will, O my God: **yea, thy law is within my heart**.

Another, "and God said…" is Coming

If we are to be mantled with His Glory, we must first know that this was *God's Intent* from the beginning. This will help us also to understand why God wants this again for us—*why He purposes to cause His Glory to be in our midst and upon our beings*.

Another, "and God said…"—is coming. This Glory encounter will come through *spoken Words*—delivered to us by the Spirit of God and received by the *Glory Carrier*. Words that have the Power to change lives and break curses. These are not ordinary Words, for they come to us with Glory substance. They are the very Words **the**

Glory Carriers will speak, revealing the Person and Power of Jesus Christ.

Amos 3:8
The lion hath roared, who will not fear? *The Lord GOD hath spoken, who can but prophesy?*

A moment to reflect:
Let's pause for a moment and reflect on the key thought, or main theme, which is the Glory of the Released or Spoken Word coming through the Glory Carrier—That is Revival.

Considering everything I have shared, God is still *pouring the Glory of His Word upon us, and into us through His Ruach HaKodesh (Holy Spirit)* (Acts 2:17). We have been given new Life in Him. We are made new creatures—and our souls redeemed from the powers of sin, death, Satan, and hell (2 Corinthians 5:17–19). Through the Holy Spirit, we have become *new bottles* that must receive and carry *the new wine of the Holy Ghost* (Matthew 9:17).

The prophet Jeremiah, moved by the Spirit, wrote: "… *I will put My law in their inward parts, and write it in their hearts;* and will be their God, and they shall be My people…for they shall all know Me, from the least of them unto the greatest of them, saith the LORD: for I will forgive their iniquity, and I will remember their sin no more (Jeremiah 31:33–34)." The Holy Spirit was describing through Jeremiah what Jesus would achieve through His ministry, death, resurrection and ascension—securing for us redemption, sanctification, and endowment through His Spirit. And the Lord continues that work through His Holy Spirit, who is at work in the Church (Ephesians 3:20). Hallelujah! I can't help but proclaim it again,

"The Glory of the released or spoken Word will speak again, through His Glory Carrier—That is Revival.

In essence, the Great Awakening Fire we long for will not come until *God speaks through His Chosen Revival Leaders.*

When God Spoke

All throughout the Bible, every time *God spoke*, powerful and wonderful things happened. Here are a few worth mentioning:

- When God spoke, Noah built an Ark that would save him and his family.
- When God spoke, a nation was started with Abraham and Sarah, and the nations of the Earth would later be blessed through their *offspring* (...that offspring is Jesus)
- When God spoke to Jacob in a dream, Jacob then named the place *Bethel*—the House of God.
- When God spoke through dreams to a seventeen-year-old Joseph, he believed the dreams were from God and would be fulfilled. Although he was hated, rejected, sold as a slave, accused of committing a crime (which he never did) and sent to prison, God was with him. That dream finally came to pass thirteen years later, when Joseph stood before Pharaoh to take up the mandate and mantle to lead a nation.
- When God spoke, He came and lit up a bush with His Fire and commissioned Moses there to *speak* to Pharaoh, to deliver Israel out of bondage.
- When God spoke, Joshua and the people obeyed His instructions, and because they did, the walls of Jericho fell.
- When God spoke, and Gideon obeyed, he was empowered and commissioned to overcome the enemy with only three hundred men.

- When God spoke, Elijah heard and obeyed, and according to the Spirit's directives, Elijah repaired the abandoned Altar of God on Mount Carmel. Then God's Fire fell. And when it did, the hearts of the people were turned back to the Lord. (More on Elijah's Mantle in a later Chapter).
- When God spoke, He laid a *prophetic pathway* through every prophet who, when *moved* by the Holy Ghost, *spoke of the Messiah and the coming Glory.*
- When Jesus spoke and commanded the disciples to wait in Jerusalem for *the coming Endowment,* the disciples heard and obeyed. Then, when *the appointed time came,* they received the Baptism of the Holy Spirit and Power.
- So now, when it comes to our turn to receive the coming Glory, God *will speak again, and keep speaking through His Chosen Vessels who carry the Glory of His Word resting on them as a MANTLE (robed with Life and Light). They will speak with the weightiness of the Word resting upon them—That is how the Church will receive the Revival Fire.*

"And God Said...

As you read through the chapters of this book, keep that *key thought* in mind: Revival is the Glory of the Word resting upon us and abiding in us. The Mantle (or, the clothing of the Anointing) is about *The Revival (or Glory) Mandate and the Mantle appointed to carry it—this is the key thought.* God mantled Adam in Genesis with the fullness of His Glory. And He still wants to give us the fullness of His Glory. **The full Glory will come.** The Spirit will Move again... And this time it will not be upon *the face of the waters, but upon the hearts of man.* And in the same order that He did in Genesis:
- He will prepare *the Way for His Word,*
- He will prepare *Hearts to receive His Spoken Word,*
- And then *He shall Speak.*

Isaiah 40:3–5

The Voice of him that crieth in the wilderness, Prepare ye the way of the LORD, make straight in the desert a highway for our God. Every valley shall be exalted, and every mountain and hill shall be made low: and the crooked shall be made straight, and the rough places plain: **And the Glory of the LORD shall be revealed, and all flesh shall see it together: for the mouth of the LORD hath spoken it.**

Ephesians 4:7

But unto every one of us is given Grace according to the measure of the Gift of Christ.

Prayer:

Speak, Lord; for our hearts are ready to receive Your glorious Fire again. "Speak Lord, for Your servant hears (1 Samuel 3:10)."

May You Be Ready To Receive The Glory Of His Word

ENDNOTES:
3. ADAMA - SOIL or EARTH (Genesis 1:7) Hebrew: אדמה
Transliteration: 'ădâmâh
Pronunciation: ad-aw-maw' Definition: From H119; soil (from its general redness): - {country} {earth} ADAM - MAN (Genesis 1:7) Hebrew: אדם
Transliteration: 'âdâm

Pronunciation: aw-dawm' Definition: From H119; {ruddy} that {is} a human being (an individual or the {species} {mankind }, Brown, F., Driver, S. R., & Briggs, C. A. (1906). The Brown-Driver-Briggs Hebrew and English Lexicon: With an Appendix Containing the Biblical Aramaic. Hendrickson Publishers, 1996 (Reprinted version)

Part 2 – Mantled for the Great Revival Mandate: the Call & Commission

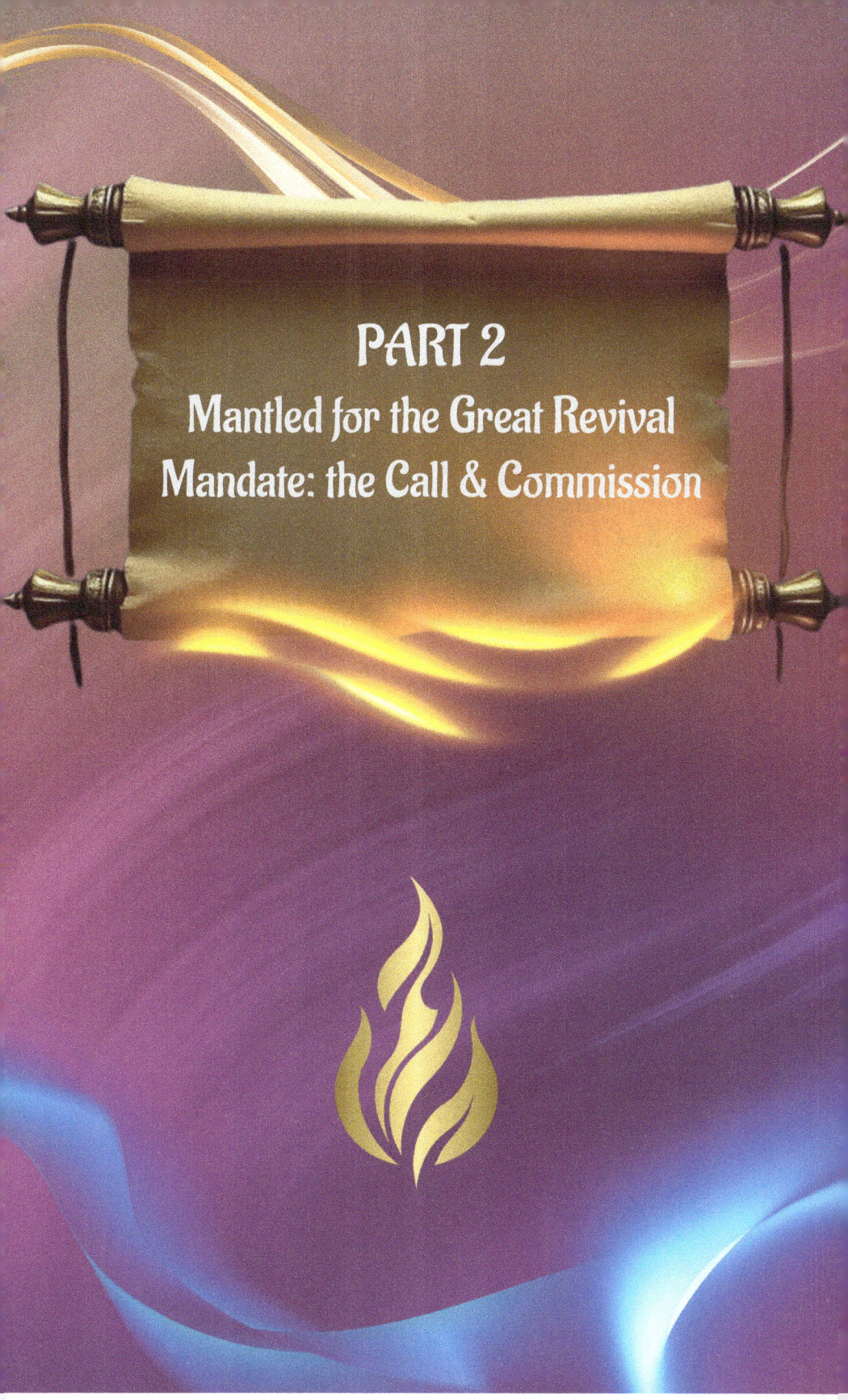

PART 2
Mantled for the Great Revival Mandate: the Call & Commission

God of the Great Revival Mandate! Come fill this Place with Your Glory

CHAPTER 2

The Great Revival Mandate

Behold, I send you!

May I present to you the theme scripture for *The Great Revival Mandate*:

Haggai 2:6–9

For thus saith the LORD of hosts; Yet once, it is a little while, and I will shake the heavens, and the earth, and the sea, and the dry land; And I will shake all nations, and the desire of all nations shall come: and I will fill this House with Glory, saith the LORD of hosts. The silver is Mine, and the gold is Mine, saith the LORD of hosts. The Glory of this latter House shall be greater than of the former, saith the LORD of hosts: and in this Place will I give Peace, saith the LORD of hosts.

As I stated earlier, a mighty and holy encounter, ordained by the Lord, is about to descend upon the Earth. *The Great Outpouring of the Glory of God is on its way.* And the Most High has ordained that a *Glory Mandate* be granted to prophetic-praying saints, postured to receive and carry *His Holy Commission.*

The Lord will shake the nations with a manifestation of His Glory not seen or felt before. (Haggai 2:6–9). The impact of *His Glory Movement* will come with immense *Heavenly Force* and will rise as a fierce tidal wave *(A Revival Wave),*[4] filled with God's Authority, Power and Compassion.

A moment to reflect:
I behold with wonder, concerning these Glory-filled visions from the Spirit. Indeed, it will be a Day of immense Power, when the Lord's Glory shall flow without reservation toward the Church. At first light, when His Revival Anthem is finally proclaimed, Love will come down and Glory will finally find His resting place. Jesus shall break through the darkness and clothe us with His First Love. Yes…First Love will be ignited in the Church and will cause us to become the reason for the shaking of the nations, for we are mantled with His Glory, Hallelujah!

Understanding the Glory Mandate

The Great Revival Mandate (or Glory Mandate) is *God's Desire and Heart for us — His People.*

Let's first define what a *Mandate* is. A mandate is an official charge, order, commission and authority given to a person or a group from a higher governing power. When someone is *mandated* to fulfil an appointed task, they are given the official authority to carry out this task. They, therefore, have the full backing, *authorisation and powers* to perform their role dutifully, carefully, diligently and correctly. They have not only been given the mandate for the task. In addition, a certain level of *knowledge* is imparted to them for the mission. The greater authority that *sends them* ensures that they are thoroughly *equipped* for their assignment (John 3:34–45).

Thus, the Great Revival *Mandate* is *the Commission* appointed to specially anointed individuals who will be used for the shaking of the nations (Haggai 2:7–9). The Mandate contains *God's Intent and Plans* about:
- Who will be used to release this Great Awakening,
- Anointings (Mantles) given to fulfil His Commission for Revival,
- Where the Great Move of God will begin,
- How the Church is to receive the fullness of His Presence. Preparatory requirements for the Church,
- Prophetic directions for the Great Outpouring and details about the Glory shaking the Church, the nations, and
- Promises that will be fulfilled.

The summarised version of the Revival Mandate includes:
- *Who* — the Vessels,
- *Through what means* — the Anointing,
- *Revival Knowledge* — Mentorship and Preparation,
- *When* — the Timing, and
- *Location* — the Place.

The Glory Mandate is the Testimony of God—Father, Son and Holy Spirit, revealed to us. It is established and carried forth by *the Spirit of Prophecy* to us (Revelation 19:10). Being more than just prophecy —it is the Heart and Mind of God revealed to those who love Him (1 Corinthians 2:9–16).

We must know what the Spirit requires from us if we truly want to enter into the *Blessing* of carrying and walking in the Baptism of His glorious *Fire*. The Spirit has sent out a *Call* to many to carry the Great Revival Mandate. He will make them ready to be used for His Glory—for the Lord desires that His Power be *visible* through them.

> **REVIVAL TRUTH:**
>
> " The Great Revival Mandate will require vessels who will *carry, lead, and serve* under a 'Commissioning Anointing' as Glory Carriers.

Commissioned to Blow the Revival Trumpet

In truth, *the Baptism of Fire* has already come upon a few and has commissioned and mantled them to go forth in the Power of God to be *witnesses and forerunners* for Him. They have been commissioned not only to *mentor* the Glory Carriers but to *blow the Trumpet* of His Revival. Like John the Baptist (Matthew 3:3), they also must announce the coming of the Great Outpouring of the Holy Spirit and say to the people of God, "Prepare ye the way of the Lord, for His Glory shall be revealed."

Isaiah 40:3–5

The voice of him that crieth in the wilderness, Prepare ye the way of the LORD, make straight in the desert a highway for our God. Every valley shall be exalted, and every mountain and hill shall be made low: and the crooked shall be made straight, and the rough places plain: **And the Glory of the LORD shall be revealed, and all flesh shall see it together: for the mouth of the LORD hath spoken it.**

Every mandate requires an appointed vessel to carry out its instructions. Thus, the Great Revival Mandate will also require vessels who will carry, lead, and serve the purpose of the Glory Mandate under a commissioning Anointing as Glory Carriers. We have this privilege given to us by the Lord to be partakers of the Great Move of God.

Adonai wants the Burning Ones to arise with the confidence of the Spirit. He wants us to know His Heart and unceasing Desire to rejuvenate and refresh His people with *the Wind of His Spirit*. The Spirit will call to us with His *Revival Trumpet*. He will be valiant for our sakes.

My Testimony of How I Received the Mantle for Revival

I believe that had I not responded to my personal call from the Lord from the very beginning, I wouldn't have reached this point of writing this book, nor would I have encountered such a magnificent heavenly thing as *the Fire of Jesus*. When these Holy Blessings were given to me, they came with a process of refining, suffering, pain, anguish, even loneliness, and much more (Romans 8:17–19). All of these for one cause—That God's Glory might be *seen and experienced again*. That Fire of God which commissions a person, also moulds him in such a way that he is never the same again. Saints, when you live a soaked life in Him, His Fire will become in you, Life-giving Waters. Often, I pinch myself concerning the grandness of the Call. I could easily say that I chose that part, but really it was He who chose me (John 15:8,16).

My first Fire Baptism experience in August 1999 did more than empower me—it transformed me. I remember then how the waves of His Glory would come to me many times after that. He was always there with me in my personal times and in the midst of the gathering of the saints. (Oh, how precious) I made a mental note that my high times in God were the moments when I found myself on my face before the Lord, worshipping Him in the early hours of the morning before sunrise. I adapted quickly to this change because the Spirit was working so powerfully in me. It didn't matter if others were with me or not. One thing mattered, and it was the Glory of His Presence in my Life. I had the audience of One, and that was all I ever wanted. On occasions, when the Waves of His Presence would wash over me, I would just sit on the floor just weeping before Him. Thus, I can say confidently, "Nothing compares to inward brokenness in His Presence. I believe that brokenness is what pleases the Lord."

And just when I thought these transformational experiences were unmatched, in February 2002, *I was anointed and commissioned by Jesus in a dream,* and the Anointing Oil from the dream was still upon my body when I woke up. The Power of that Anointing is beyond any words, and to this day, it's still ineffable—I remember at that time it left me overwhelmed and pondering deeply on what would become of me. In the dream, it was Jesus who introduced the ANOINTING and the GREAT REVIVAL MANDATE to me. Thus, it is true that we do not choose our Callings or Anointings; Jesus chooses them for us (John 15:8,16). When Jesus anointed me in the dream, He said specific Words that have left a Divine hallmark in my spirit. It was in the same dream that the Holy Spirit used three key words that you will find me using throughout the book—Anointed to be the **Carrier, Leader and Servant** of the Great Work.[5-6]

In May of 2012, I then encountered Jesus' Baptismal Fire again in a vision. At that time, I was desperate for the Lord again. I can testify that when an individual decides to pursue God, they don't actually know that God is already postured to come to them. And that's exactly what the Lord did for me. He came and consumed me with His Fire, and it burned so wonderfully upon my being. Is that your cry today? You can make it yours even now, as I say it... "Baptise me with Your Fire, oh God."

I have continued to experience His Revival Fire in my life. If it weren't so, I wouldn't have said it. I believe that to be soaked in seasons of worshipping Him is to be soaked in the beauty and magnificence of His Glory. *Soak in Him*, oh beloved of the Lord—that is the place to be.

Now, such an Anointing doesn't come without moulding, suffering and tribulation. And I have had my fair share of that. When you have been *marked by the Fire of God* in such a way, and then go through a moulding beyond your capacity to understand it, you know that it is the *Zeal of God at work, and* you realise eventually that this is the life He has chosen for you—not for yourself, but for Him. Therefore, the Baptismal Fire doesn't just ignite you; He does a good and great work in you. Will you be moulded for His Glory? That was the case for me, and still is today. I see it now in hindsight, that from encounter to encounter, little did I know that such a God-pursuit would come with it pain, loss, failure, moulding, maturing and growth. This refining process was to break me down to the point that I had no clue where I was going, yet I learnt to trust in Him. All I had was total dependency on Him. That is the most important aspect of life *hidden in Christ—to be totally dependent on His Spirit.* What might have looked like *blind dependency* was actually the sovereign work of God happening so profoundly in my life. And if you want such an Anointing as the

PART 2   *Mantled for the Great Revival Mandate: the Call & Commission*

Revival Anointing, you must also welcome the moulding that comes with it.

> "It is a necessary work by the Holy Spirit to be moulded so that you can be made ready to host and release His Fire.

For more of my story:
Read my book 'Chosen to Carry the Glory—Carry the Fire of Jesus.'

The Revival Fire is God's promise to you. Know that you are the remnant He has chosen: to be *washed* by the Blood of the Lamb (Revelation 19:6–9), and *endowed* with the Power of His Testimony (Revelation 12:11). *For your place is to be His House*—to *host* and *reveal* the Glory of *Yahweh* (Haggai 2:6–9). Therefore, oh chosen of the Lord, take courage and let your heart look unto the Glory of God. I conclude this chapter with the words of the famous song by Helen Lemmel (1918), "Turn your eyes upon Jesus, look full in His wonderful Face, and the things of Earth will grow strangely dim, in the Light of His Glory and Grace."[7]

Prayer:
Jesus, our Lord and Saviour, pour Your Glory upon us like the Anointing Oil. Oh, let our oneness with You cause Your Glory to abide in our midst. We say Yes, Lord. We say yes to Your Great Awakening Fire, Amen…

May You Receive the Blessing of His Glory In Your Midst!

ENDNOTES:

4.	Sabadi, N.M.T, 2023. Chapter 4 Our Heritage—Endued with Power, Jesus—Led by Spirit, *Chosen to Carry the Glory—Carry the Fire of Jesus,* Norman Sabadi Publishing, Rockhampton, Queensland, Australia p.17).

5.	Sabadi, N.M.T, 2023. Chapter 10 The Great Induction & Anointing Service, *Chosen to Carry the Glory—Carry the Fire of Jesus,* Norman Sabadi Publishing, Rockhampton, Queensland, Australia pp.157-174).

6.	Sabadi, N.M.T, 2023. Chapter 19 The Place Where He Speaks, *Chosen to Carry the Glory —Carry the Fire of Jesus,* Norman Sabadi Publishing, Rockhampton, Queensland, Australia pp.319-321).

7.	Lemmel, Helen H. Turn Your Eyes Upon Jesus. 1918. In Glad Songs, 192

'Behold, I have set before thee an OPEN DOOR.'

CHAPTER 3

The Mighty Release of Mantles

Mantled With His Glory.

John 3:27
John answered and said, A man can receive nothing, except it be given him from Heaven.

The Mantle is God's authorisation to move in the Holy Ghost, yet every step must be guided by Him. This authority flows only as we yield completely to the Holy Spirit. From the moment you receive your appointed Mantle, you have special privileges in the Spirit, to move—and be moved. You don't need a man's approval or permission for this. The Mantle takes effect immediately as it endows you. With it are the gifts of the Spirit, which begin to operate in and through you as God's vessel of honour.

The Mantle is foundational because encounter with God is foundational. If you have received a Burning Bush or Upper Room kind of experience, that too is foundational, as it is God's Commission—and He does not require man's permission to function through you. *Commission is permission.* The Mantle endows you with God's language of breakthrough. God speaks, representing Himself. And so, the language you receive with the Mantle doesn't need anyone's permission or endorsement to be spoken. You can't deny the supernatural nature of the Mantle because its impact is caused by God Himself. God's Mantle is His Person and Power.

> "It's not the man, but the man with the Mantle that speaks with God's Power.

And, while the Mantle rests on you, its supernatural workings will cause you to receive more from the Spirit so that **He can do more in you and through you.**

The Mantle is Postured for Revival

The Mantle (is the Anointing that clothes a person). It has specific traits and is given by the Holy Ghost. The Revivalist Mantle is positioned and postured to honour the Lord so that the one who wears it is girded with the intent to fulfil God's Holy Mandate—to release His Glory upon the nations.

When *the Mantle Moves* into position (or as the prophets of old described it, when the Spirit of the Lord came upon them) the vessel takes on more of *the personality and attitude of Jesus Christ*. The man with the Mantle then has access to God, because the Mantle is evidence of the Holy Spirit at work in us (Ephesians 3:20). A Revivalist will do nothing else except obey the *Directive* of the Anointing resting upon him to release God's Glory. He is mantled with the Glory Mandate. Thus, it is natural and characteristic of him to give his full attention to the Holy Spirit and the Power endowed upon him by the Mantle. Hallelujah!

The Mantle of the Glory Carrier is an 'OPEN DOOR'

> **REVIVAL TRUTH:**
> " The Glory Carrier is God's Watchman at the City Gates. He is God's Open Door for the Glory to enter.

Now, the Mantle of the Glory Carrier is an OPEN DOOR Mantle —*opened by the LORD,* and no man can shut it.

Revelation 3:7–8

And to the angel of the church in Philadelphia write; These things saith He that is Holy, He that is True, He that hath the key of David, He that openeth, and no man shutteth; and shutteth, and no man openeth; I know thy works: behold, I have set before thee an open door, and no man can shut it: for thou hast a little strength, and hast kept My Word, and hast not denied My Name.

The Lord always provides for Himself, an *open door or an ancient gate (a metonymy or metaphor for a Revivalist). That Open Door is a man after God's Heart* (1 Samuel 13:14, 16:1).

The mantling for the Great Revival Mandate is written clearly in Psalms 24, and a specific reference mentions what I call *the open-*

door vessel. Psalms 24 reveals the *open-door Mantle resting upon the Glory Carrier.*

Psalms 24:3–10

Who shall ascend into the Hill of the LORD? or who shall stand in His Holy Place? He that hath clean hands, and a pure heart; who hath not lifted up his soul unto vanity, nor sworn deceitfully. He shall receive the Blessing from the LORD, and righteousness from the God of his salvation. This is the generation of them that seek Him, that seek Thy Face, O Jacob. Selah. *Lift up your heads, O ye gates; and be ye lift up, ye everlasting doors;* and the King of Glory shall come in. Who is this King of Glory? The LORD strong and mighty, the LORD mighty in battle. Lift up your heads, O ye gates; even lift them up, ye everlasting doors; and the King of Glory shall come in. Who is this King of Glory? The LORD of hosts, He is the King of Glory. Selah

Friends, if you learn to walk consciously of the Holy Spirit by honouring the sanctity of His Words in you, and by guarding your heart with all diligence, you will have access to Him and become *an Ancient Gate* chosen by the Lord to reveal His Glory. For the Spirit also pursues the hearts of those who pursue Him. He *honours their honouring* of Him, and He *marks them with His Revival-carrying Mantle* so that they can be God's open door for encounter.

> "Friends of God, you must have an open-door worship posture to receive His Glory.

Glory Carriers are God's *open doors,* and open doors *do not* shut God out—they never limit, hinder, restrict, suppress, or reject the Holy Spirit. They are God's *Ancient Gates*—(Remembering that this was the original design of man—to illuminate God's Glory) And when God opens these chosen doors, they *remain open* (Revelation 3:7–8).

An additional thought:
When you pray for an "Open Heaven," you're asking God to look upon an *Open Door* (A Revivalist) and to come through *His Revivalist* to release His Glory upon the people. An Open Heaven can only happen when you acknowledge the *Portal or Open Door* by which God enters a room. *An Open Door is the portal that creates an Open Heaven* (Isaiah 66:1-2). Revivalists Carry God's Atmosphere and Influence wherever they go, and when they stand in a Place and *open their mouth to speak, then God will speak through them.* The Place from which God speaks is not only Heaven, but also in and through a chosen vessel—one who has made his life a Place of God's Rest and Abode.

Unique Mantles Assigned to Nations

I am anticipating a great Glory-shaking that will be felt throughout the Earth. Hallelujah! There will also be Mantles assigned to nations, as the Spirit pours His Glory upon them. From prophetic Words that I have received, I believe that Papua New Guinea will be mantled as God's Appointed Fire Starter and Leader of the Move of God. Australia will wear a Mantle of Worship and prophetic songs. As the Great South Land of the Holy Ghost, Australia will lead the nations in worship. Fiji is called the Rising

Star of God—abundant with worshippers and abundant in good works. (These Mantles have deeper meanings). I know of these three nations for now, and I believe other prophets have received Words for their respective nations. Each nation has a part to play in the Great Awakening Fire of God. Many nations will raise the prophetic Banner of Revival. The Lord has appointed that the Glory of His *Latter House—which is the Church—*be greater than that of the *Former House.*

Malachi 1:11

For from the rising of the sun even unto the going down of the same My Name shall be great among the Gentiles; and *in every place* incense shall be offered unto My Name, and a pure offering: for My Name shall be great *among the heathen*, saith the LORD of hosts.

A Mighty Release of Mantles

> **REVIVAL TRUTH:**
> "The saints shall be mantled with His Glory

I believe that there shall be a *great release of Mantles* as the Spirit moves upon His people with His Revival Fire. He will not just hover over us, He will *speak His Glory into us and through us*. The words, "Not by might, nor by power, but by My Spirit" (Zechariah 4:6), will echo throughout the Earth, as Holy Ghost Mantles are released upon God's people across the Earth. The Wind of the Spirit will blow, and with it, the raising of new prophetic Revival

Leaders. There are, and will be, an ever-increasing measure of Mantles. Mantles of worship, Mantles of the prophets, Mantles for business and wealth, Mantles of the apostles, Mantles of mighty evangelists like Philip, Mantles of weighty teaching, Mantles to preach, and Mantles to make war with the enemy and win the victory. **The saints shall be mantled with His Glory.** Not many understand this, but a part of *the Elijah-Spirit-and-Power Commission* is to mantle the Saints. *God anoints us for Himself.* We are not anointed for us, we are anointed for *Him*—we are mantled with His Glory.

Not My Will But Yours Be Done

Crush me, Lord, till Your Oil flows.
Not my will but Yours be done.

Jesus prayed with exceeding sorrow and grief in the Garden of *Gethsemane*. *Gethsemane* means the Crushing (Olive) Oil Press. Indeed, Christ (the Anointed One) was being crushed for us, and the anguish of that crushing already began in the Olive Garden. He was going to endure suffering. He had already mentioned this to the disciples that He would suffer many terrible things and be rejected by the elders and later be put to death (Luke 9:22).

The scene that took place in the Garden of Gethsemane was one of *pure love for us* (Matthew 26:36–44, Luke 22:41–46). Jesus fell on His Face, and He prayed with great anguish, "Oh My Father, if it be possible, let this cup (of suffering and death) pass from me: nevertheless, not My will, but as You will." After checking on His disciples, He went and fell on His Face and prayed again, "If You are willing, take this cup from Me. Nevertheless, not My will, but Yours be done." Then an angel from Heaven was there to strengthen Him (Luke 22:43). Jesus, (God's Chief Revivalist) showed us how to be God's OPEN DOOR—as the Carrier, Leader and Servant of His Father's Will. Glory Carriers also carry the same attitude and heart posture. They say to the Lord, "Not my will but Yours be done." That crushing must happen because the *Oil of His Purpose must flow from us to the Church.* The crushing is necessary. I note with great awe concerning this wonderful insight that the Revelation 3:7–8 passage is actually our Lord Jesus speaking (He who was the example of what it means to be crushed so the Oil would pour forth). Jesus was addressing the Church about *the open door Mandate.*

To my mind, the pure excellence of this astonishingly amazing revelation is beyond natural-level comprehension. Our Lord Jesus Christ is the King of Glory *(Melech HaKavod)* referenced in Psalms 24: *He was the* one who showed us how to have clean hands and a pure heart so that we too can ascend to the Hill of Glory. And now He is telling us "Behold, I have set before thee an open door, and no man can shut it: for thou hast a little strength, and hast kept My Word, and hast not denied My Name."

The Mind of God amazes me. For God sent His only Son, Jesus, to be the example of what it means to be an open door vessel. Now it is our turn. We are that generation (spoken of in Psalms 24:6) who are postured to receive Jesus, the King of Glory. Hallelujah! We are His Temple, founded upon the Messiah, Jesus our Lord, our Cornerstone. For He shall do the same mighty work in us.

> "Jesus Christ, the King of Glory, shall come through His Revivalists—His Ancient Gates and Everlasting Doors—to release His Glory upon the nations.

With this in mind, know that the Revival Mantle comes with a moulding to build maturity, deeper willingness, and readiness in those chosen to walk in, and with this special Anointing. We must also go through our *Gethsemane* so that the Holy Spirit's Power, working through His endowed Mantle, can then flow through us to heal the nations (Zechariah 4). Jesus demonstrated for us that it is important to humble ourselves and to yield the Father's Will. We, therefore, must also be willing to go through our moulding, which is God's plan for us to be equipped through *Mentorship* and *Discipline, for His Cause.*

The best part about this is that we are anointed *for Him,* and not for ourselves. We are mantled with *His Glory*—for His Glory... Amen.

Prayer:
...Nevertheless, not my will Lord, but Yours be done... Amen.

May You Be His Open Door and Ancient Gate, for the King of Glory to Enter!

Part 3 – The Preparatory Moves & Mentorship for the Move

"I will instruct thee and teach thee in the way which thou shalt go: I will guide thee with Mine Eye."
—Psalms 32:8

CHAPTER 4

Mentorship: The Prerequisite for the Move of God

The Church will not be able to enter the Move without Holy Spirit-guided Mentorship.

Holy-Spirit-led Move requires a Spirit-initiated, Spirit-led Mentorship. Only the Holy Spirit can help us enter into the Move correctly (1 Corinthians 2:9–13). The Move of God requires Revival Mentors, not just ministers. Because the Move of God has a prerequisite—Discipleship by the Baptismal Fire of God. As Jesus knew and told His disciples, that without the Spirit's counsel we have no *Guide to teach, comfort and lead us*. The Church will not be able to enter the Revival Fire without *specific Revival Mentorship*. Nor will the Church, as a whole, be able to accommodate the New in God if the Church refuses to be mentored for the Glory.

John 6:63
It is the Spirit that quickeneth; the flesh profiteth nothing: the Words that I speak unto you, they are Spirit, and they are Life.

Mentorship is Discipleship—where the Holy Spirit imparts to us *the Knowledge of the Glory of the Lord* (Isaiah 11:9, Habakkuk 2:14, Ephesians 1:9,17–20). Jesus did say that when the Spirit of Truth comes, *He will guide us into all Truth.* So if we are going to be postured to receive the Glory, then we must first be willing to receive Revival Truths that teach us how to *receive and host the Glory* (John 16:13–15).

The Church Lacks Revival Knowledge

Despite this significant Truth about the forthcoming Glory, *the posture* to receive *this blessed Promise* has not yet been fully understood in the Church. Revival knowledge has to first be deeply embedded before it can become a reality in everyday life and Christian ministry.

That said, I note that a Pharisee-like spirit is fighting against the Church to stop her from seeing the importance of the Revival Mandate. This is the work of demons, wanting to keep the Church blind or stuck in a religious rut—never breaking free to experience Revival Knowledge. Plainly put, the gates of hell fear one thing: that once the Church understands and embraces her place in the Revival Mandate, God's people will rise as a spiritual force to be reckoned with.

I have personally seen the lack of Revival-Knowledge openly displayed at prayer meetings and even preached from pulpits. At first, I thought I was overreacting, but my ongoing observations reinforced my convictions about how so many saints are asking for

Revival, preaching about their hunger for it, but not actually knowing how to receive and host Revival Fire. If they only understood that the Spirit is already ready to work in their midst and is waiting for them to recognise Him. He is waiting for them to understand how to receive and host Him. I observe, meeting after meeting, the same versions of prayers and messages asking God for Revival. And it's not that the Holy Spirit hasn't heard our cries for Revival. In fact, the Spirit is actually waiting for us to respond correctly. The missing component is for us *to know and flow with His Glory in our midst.*

> **REVIVAL TRUTH:**
>
> " Revival Power is never void of Revival Revelation. You can't have Revival Power without Revival Revelation.

Also, many saints want to carry a Revival Anointing, but they do not know how *to recognise the Anointing.* Most seek after God with genuine passion. But passion without knowledge is equivalent to an apprentice seeking to become a master, yet refusing the lessons that lead to the achievement of mastery.

A commentary from another fellow minister:
It's like wanting to fly a fighter jet. It's that powerful and that dangerous at the same time that if you just state your intent and then proceed to climb into the flight deck and take off, at worst, you'll crash and burn. At best, you'll not go anywhere (because you don't know how to fly a jet).

The truth of the matter is that many are praying for what they don't fully know or understand. It's one thing to pray for the Move of God. It's another thing to know how to host the Glory in your midst. In fact, many are looking for an encounter with God, but they have not been taught how to receive holy encounters. From my observations, when there is a haphazard pursuit of Revival or a lack of true discipleship for *Revival Knowledge*, there is just no hosting of the Glory. We can't deny this anymore or cover it up with outward pretence. This *knowledge deficit* or *ignorance crisis* is real. Sadly, many leaders and ministers still strive with actions and programs that are counterintuitive to their own prayers for Revival. This inconsistency is quite bewildering. Many pray for an encounter with God, yet their actions betray them—for deep down, they would rather not be interrupted if that encounter disrupts their schedules and programs. I see in this a *great disconnect*—that they proclaim with their mouths, "Lord, send Revival," but their hearts are far from *the true meaning of Revival* (Isaiah 29:13–14)—the kind of Revival that comes in God's timing, with a Spirit-breathed shaking and shifting of hearts and minds.

> **REVIVAL TRUTH:**
>
> " You have to first be "A disciple of Revival" before you can be made "A mentor of Revival."

The behaviour of some leaders toward the Holy Spirit is the hindrance here. You can't leave the Holy Ghost outside of your gatherings by being overly cautious and restrictive and then expect Him to move in your meetings. It's absurd to want a Move but refuse *the Mover*; to be hungry for the Move, but not recognise or know the *Voice of the Move*; to ask for His Presence, and then reject *the manifestation* of His Presence.

My fellow ministers, this Holy-Ghost-led mentorship is God's initiative for all of us. I encourage you to let go of your concept of the Move and let Him enter the Room. The Holy Spirit knows what must be done, and you do well to obey Him—for He is the Power at work in us. (Ephesians 3:20).

The Revivalist—the Mentor of Revival

Two examples of Old Testament discipleship worth noting were Moses's discipleship of Joshua and Elijah's discipleship of Elisha. Moses and Elijah were leaders of the Move of God, *picked* by God, *anointed* by God, and *led* by God. I love that the specifics of mentorship are also ordained in God's Revival Plan. Elisha received a level of mentorship that was peculiar to the Anointing that rested upon his mentor, Elijah. This was the case with Joshua, who also served Moses as a faithful steward (More on Joshua in a later Chapter).

Likewise, you have to first be a *disciple* of Revival before you can be made a *mentor* of Revival. That's how Jesus also operated. He mentored disciples and trained them to walk with Him. Before they ever became *Carriers of the Fire*, they first became *Disciples of the Fire*. In the same way, you have to first be a willing student of the Move of God before you become a dedicated mentor of the Move. You can't be a *Father of the Move*, unless you first submit as a son to the Spirit and be discipled by your Heavenly Father.

A high point:
The Spirit will mentor you through a Revivalist-father, and God will appoint this person for you. This Revivalist-father has already been walking with the Lord and knows how to host the Glory of God.

As a disciple of Revival, you must be taught how to behold the Word, and how to host the Glory of the Word that enters your spirit —that is Revival. You must first be a disciple of Revival if you want to carry the Glory. Then, when the Word of Revival has been *conceived in you,* the Holy Ghost will posture you to be *God's spiritual Bethlehem—the appointed birthplace* of the Move of God. As God's *spiritual Bethlehem,* we are called to *receive* and *release* the Move. The Light of God's Glory must rise upon us, and shine bright through us (Isaiah 60:1–3).

Jesus gave us the revelation of mentorship (discipleship) when He began His Ministry. *He came to write the Word in our hearts.* When Jesus began mentoring, the process started by selecting individuals to be *His disciples.* These handpicked few later became Glory Carriers and Witnesses of the Power of the Gospel of Christ—when the Spirit came upon them in the Upper Room (Acts 2:1–4). Because that was what Jesus wanted for them—to be Witnesses for Him (Acts 1:8). And Jesus has continued His mentorship through the Holy Spirit—the same Holy Spirit who searches the deep things of God and knows the Mind of God, and reveals to us all Truth (John 14:26, 1 Corinthians 2:10–12).

John 8:31–32

Then said Jesus to those Jews which believed on Him, If ye continue in My Word, then are ye My disciples indeed; And ye shall know the Truth, and the Truth shall make you free.

For our Lord to impart what He was carrying, He first had to mentor the disciples—*under His Glory Carriers Mentorship.* This mentoring took time—over three years of careful attention. He made sure that the disciples would be aligned and positioned to receive *the Glory Mandate.* The final instruction from the Lord Jesus to His disciples came before His departure. That instruction was a *positioning to receive* the Power from on High. Jesus blew a *Spiritual Revival Trumpet* when He told the disciples to return to Jerusalem and wait for the Promise of the Outpouring of the Spirit.

Then came *the Day of Pentecost (Acts 2)*. I call it the disciples' *Graduation Day*. Because as soon as the Spirit came upon them, they went from ordinary believers to *Fire-Carrying Witnesses*. Christ's mentorship was imperative for this to happen. As a part of the discipleship to carry the Glory, He made it clear to them that it was necessary for Him to return to the Father—this would initiate the sending of the Holy Spirit (Acts 1:4-8). Also, Jesus didn't just instruct them to wait in Jerusalem; He also gave them the *Commission (the Mandate) ahead of time* (Matthew 28:18-20). Connecting the two elements—There was the instruction to wait for the Power (for them to be mantled), and there was *the Mandate assigned with the Mantles.*

Therefore, a Revival-leader with clear direction from the Holy Spirit wears a Mantle with an assigned Mandate.

"Every Mantle has an assigned Mandate… No Mantle is ever without a Mandate.

Additional thoughts:
Every Mantle is unique, because every Mandate is unique. The vessel is also specifically picked to wear the Mantle—to carry-lead-serve the Mantle and its assigned Mandate.

Christ—the Foundation of the Move

"Christ is the foundation of the Move and the Cornerstone of the Church.

I pray that you also see the importance of the pattern laid out for us by Jesus to the early Church. Jesus said to the apostle Peter that He would establish *His Testimony*. "Simon, son of Jona, you are

Peter—Rock, and upon this Rock, I shall build My Church" (Matthew 16:13–19). This wasn't just a wonderful declaration over Peter, it was *prophecy with a Promise* to be fulfilled. The Rock of God —Jesus Christ, revealed the Rock Message. Jesus made it known that He is *the foundation of the Move,* and *the Cornerstone of the Church* (Psalms 118:21–21, Acts 4:11–12). Peter would later fulfil the meaning of that name as a part of his mandate *at an appointed place and time* (Acts 2:14). This was to be the Rock Message—*the founding Revival Message to the Church.* And so it was, when the Day of the Promised Endowment of Power had come, it was Peter who stood up and girded with a Revival Mantle, preached *the inaugural message* of the Church, "It shall come to pass in the last days that *I shall pour out My Spirit* upon all flesh, and your sons and daughters shall *prophesy…*" (Acts 2:14–41).

The disciples were endowed with Power and became Fire Carriers from that moment onward. It wasn't just Power *witnessed,* but Power *present to witness.* The effectiveness, revelation and impact of the Mantle were at work. For while the Spirit rested on them, He also continued to mentor them effectively. And they responded, received and released.

The principle of Revival Mentorship stems from this: they were clothed with the Fire of Christ only because they were willing—for as long as it took—to sit at the Feet of Jesus, the Mentor of Revival. They learnt *the ways* of the Revivalist by observing Jesus—their Mentor and Father. Now, it was their turn. The disciples weren't only Carriers of the Great Move, but were made spiritual fathers, who fathered by example. They were ready to lead the Church into *Greater Works* for the glory of God.

Thus, on this foundation, I confidently say to you, "It's now your turn to be *mentored* by the Spirit of Revival Truth."

Prayer:
Holy Spirit, we submit to Your Revival Mentorship. We are ready to receive the Great Revival Fire. In Yeshua's Holy Name, Amen…

May Adonai's Mentorship Prepare You To Receive the Day of the Great Awakening!

"I will shake the nations, and the desire of all nations shall come: and I will fill this House with My Glory," Says the Lord of Hosts

CHAPTER 5

The Preliminary Revival Fires Are Already Here

*We are called to witness and become
the reason for the shaking of the nations.*

The Revival Fire is not meant to be a one-time event but a continuous living experience with the Glory of God. These continuous encounters are *God's initial Fires* purposed to get the saints ready for the greatest and most historic event ever—*the Great Outpouring of God's Glory*. Now, the fact that these *initial Moves* are small in their impact, compared to the coming Great Awakening, does not in any way water down their efficacy or purpose. They are necessary and intended to cause God's people to be ready to receive the coming Great Move. When we humbly accept the purpose of the ongoing *preparatory Moves*, we align ourselves to His Will and are made ready to receive the Day of the Great Outpouring. Therefore, we must treat these *initial preparatory Moves* with the same level of reverence and honour. We must not reject the *preliminary workings* of the Spirit in our midst. Otherwise, we will grieve the Holy Spirit of God (1 Thessalonians 5:21).

God: the Author & Initiator of the Move

> **REVIVAL TRUTH:**
>
> " Revival does not come from man but from the Living God.

The Glory-Day is approaching, and the attempts by many zealous ministers to fulfil this highly anticipated *Event* have led to individuals thinking they can kindle God's Move by their efforts. In doing so, they disregard and reject specific *Holy-Spirit-led Revival mentorship* intended for the Church. Many have attempted to force a *birthing* when there is no need to do so. The truth is, only God is the *Author and Ignitor-Initiator* of His Move. This is *His initiative—for us. Not ours—for Him.*

So, if we want the Move of God, we must first learn to surrender to the Holy Ghost. He is the Leader of the Move. Only He can *guide and ignite* the Fire that must be received by the Church. He knows how He wants to give this *Great Blessing* to us. We can try as much as we want to create a move, but we are nothing without Him (John 15:1-4). In truth, we will labour in vain when God is not *the Leader of His Move* (Psalms 127:1). However, when we submit to His leadership, that's when we are led to fulfil His Revival Mandate correctly.

God's Gideon Army

The Spirit of God is already in the process of raising a *Gideon Army* of selected individuals. This is that generation whose heart has chosen to pursue the Face of God and to seek after His Presence (Psalms 24:6). They do not want the garments of religious practices, nor the binding rules of churchianity. Rather, they have chosen to walk with the Holy Spirit (Galatians 5:25). They no longer want the programs that water down the Move of God. They refuse to be led astray from His Presence. They want a *Holy Encounter* with the Glory of God. They don't want to just be present to make numbers and warm seats. These *Hungry Ones* have confidently entered into the Holy of Holies where God, in all His Glory, wants to meet with them and commune with them (Exodus 25:22). They have set their gaze upon the Holy One and have waited with patience for the rising of the dawn of His Glory. They are His Sheep and they know His Voice (John 10:27). They are willing to linger and lean towards Him, to be *mentored* so that they are *ready to receive* the Day of the Lord's Great Awakening. Hallelujah! The Dawn of the New Day of God's Fire is already at work in them, and boldness from the Holy Ghost is growing upon them to be a fiery and fearless generation of Glory Carriers.

> **REVIVAL TRUTH:**
>
> " The preliminary Revival Fires are already here.

Prayer:
Come and ignite us with Your Revival Fire, oh Lord, and do a mighty work in us. We are ready to receive the Glory of Your Word. In Jesus' Name, Amen...

May You Be Ready For the Day of the Great Awakening!

The Preliminary Revival Fires are Already Here   CHAPTER 5

Part 4 – The Birth of the Great Move
(Prophetic Foundations)

PART 4
The Birth of the Great Move
(Prophetic Foundations)

'The Church shall conceive and give birth to the Great Move of God'

CHAPTER 6

The Ordained Birth of the Great Awakening is at Hand

"My Church shall conceive and give birth to the Move I have chosen," says the Lord.

Genesis 21:1–2
And the LORD visited Sarah as He had said, and the LORD did unto Sarah as He had spoken. For Sarah conceived, and bare Abraham a son in his old age, at the set time of which God had spoken to him.

At the end of May 2021, the Lord instructed us to host a conference for Him in Cairns City. It was during a day session of the seven-day conference, when the Word of the Lord came to me, and the Spirit said to me, "*Sarah* shall conceive: *My Church shall conceive and give birth to the Promise* I have made (for the Great Revival). For the *zeal* of the Lord shall perform this." Then the Spirit said, "The Mantle of Joseph, *My deliverer*, has come. Joseph, My Joseph!" As the Word came to me, I immediately prostrated before the Lord, Holy Spirit and received His Word.

Conceive and *birth*? Yes, indeed. Such powerful Words from the Holy Ghost. That is what the Spirit of God is going to do in each of you. He wants *His Abiding Word* to rest upon you.

When the glorious Power of God comes and rests upon earthen vessels, the Lord's Holy Mandate is *conceived* and then *birthed at the appointed time and the appointed place*. That holy Baptism of Fire that rests upon chosen vessels becomes in them a fiery Move of God that cannot be contained. With that fiery Anointing is God's *Revival Assignment*, which was conceived in the vessel and carried to full term, to the time of its birth. When the Glory of *the Abiding Word* is conceived in these chosen vessels, you will notice that the boldness of the Spirit of Christ will be evident in their proclamation of Him, through the way they carry themselves and speak. I believe it is the Power of the Mantle responding to the Word conceived in them by the Holy Ghost.

This is just like when Mary, the mother of Jesus, accepted her part in the *Plan* of God and said to the angel that delivered the Word, "Be it unto me according to Your Word." For as soon as she came into agreement with the Plan and Purpose of Heaven, *the Move of God was conceived in her by the Holy Ghost* (Luke 1:27–38). And like Mary, when you also come into agreement with the Plan and Purpose of Heaven, the Move of God is then conceived in your spirit by the Holy Ghost.

The Lord Jesus, before departing to Heaven, had commanded the disciples to go and wait in Jerusalem for the Promise of the Holy Spirit (Acts 1:4–8). As soon as *they believed the Word from the Mouth of Christ*, the Word for Revival was conceived in them. And, a few days after, they would experience the living Presence of the Glory of Christ's Words.

> **REVIVAL TRUTH:**
>
> " When you come into agreement with the Plan and Purpose of Heaven, the Move of God is then conceived in your spirit by the Holy Ghost.

When the disciples returned to Jerusalem, they gathered together in the Upper Room. They waited, prayed, fasted, and communed with one another. Their hearts were in one accord with the Holy Spirit, and they were ready to receive the fullness of *the Blessing* of the Father (Acts 2:1–4). Then, when *the appointed time* had come, the Power of the Spirit descended and rested mightily upon the saints. There, in that *appointed place,* the hundred and twenty saints were clothed with the Fire of the Holy Ghost and God's mighty Move was *birthed*. They were filled and overflowing with the Power from on High (John 7:38–39, Acts 1:4,8).

As I sit in His Presence and meditate upon this wonderful revelation of the Move of God, I am in awe of Him. How marvellous it is that He has chosen us to be a part of the appointed Day of the Birth of the Move and to carry His Holy Mandate to the nations. Oh, that you would discern God's *Desire* for you; for *He wants to birth a mighty Move through you also*. Will you make yourself available to be used for the Lord's purpose?

When God's Move is birthed through us as the Fire Carriers, it changes the spiritual positioning, authority and effectiveness of our Churches. This transformation then spills over and affects the spiritual DNA of the city in which that Church abides. When the Great Revival Fire comes, the Lord will change the spiritual DNA of villages, towns, and cities. The transformation will be so significant that it will change the culture of that region to a *God Culture*. And this will happen only when we surrender completely to the *leadership* of the Holy Spirit.

> **REVIVAL TRUTH:**
>
> " The Spirit pursues the hearts of those who pursue Him. He honours their honouring of Him.

Also, in the lead-up to the release of the Revival Fire, a hunger for the Move will grip the Church. This hunger is part of the inner workings of the Holy Ghost, and it will be persistent in those who have been stirred by the Spirit until it becomes *the worship posture* that makes room for the Glory to come and abide. A part of this conviction is to identify and make room for the Fire Carriers, who have begun to demonstrate a heightened level of awareness toward the Holy Spirit. These individuals have understood that God's Desire is for them to know Him more. And because of their awareness of the Abiding Word in the Room, *the Assigned Revival Fire* has been *placed in them*. These Fire-carrying individuals will then be used as the ushers of the Move and *as God's prophetic confrontation*, which will work in the Church early to prepare the Church's posture. This will all build in momentum and intensity until a threshold or climax in the Spirit is reached. Only then shall the appointed time be upon us, when the Church shall finally receive the glorious *release* of the Great Move of God.

This is like when the Word of the Lord came to Abraham and Sarah, about Sarah's conceiving and giving birth to the promised Isaac (Genesis 21:1–2). That's exactly what the Spirit is doing right now. He is preparing the Church to conceive and give birth to the Move. And to achieve this, the Word of Glory must first find *His resting place*—a vessel that trembles at His Word (Isaiah 66:1–2). And from that resting place, the Fire of God flows as Rivers of Life (John 7:38). At the break of dawn, the *Birth* of the Great Move of the Spirit will come to us early, Hallelujah (Psalms 46:1–5)!

As I continue to behold this amazing revelation (as a witness in my spirit), how can I reject or make light of the *Holy Invitation* of the Lord Holy Spirit? For I have given myself to receiving His Manifested Word. And, I believe this *Invitation* is open to all those who will respond to it with all their heart, mind and soul. The prophet, Moses, was exactly this way before God (Exodus 33 and 34). God had invited him to ascend to *the place* that the Lord God had prepared for him. It would be at *the appointed place* and at *the appointed time* that God would show His Glory to Moses. (Note the bolded text)

Exodus 33:18-23

And he said, I beseech thee, shew me Thy Glory. And He said, I will make all My Goodness pass before thee, and I will proclaim the Name of the LORD before thee; and will be gracious to whom I will be gracious, and will shew mercy on whom I will shew mercy. And He said, Thou canst not see My Face: for there shall no man see Me, and live. **And the LORD said, Behold, there is a place by Me, and thou shalt stand upon a rock:** And it shall come to pass, while My Glory passeth by, that I will put thee in a Clift of the rock, and will cover thee with My Hand while I pass by: And I will take away Mine Hand, and thou shalt see My Back Parts: but My Face shall not be seen.

And just as God did with Moses, He shall also do the same for us. The Lord God also invites you to His Holy Place. Will you ascend to the Holy Hill of the Lord to *the appointed place* by the cleft of the Rock (The Place of His Presence—The Place Where He Speaks)? It's time for you to behold the *Abiding Word*. It's time for the Move of God to be conceived in you. *The appointed Isaac* (The promised Great Move of God) has already been planned, and a Mandate to carry this child to term has also been assigned. For God is going to cause *Sarah* (the Church) to give birth to *this promised Blessing*.

Now that you are aware of this, I must also state clearly that we cannot, by our strength or works, fulfil this *promised Isaac—it is of the Holy Ghost, and not of man*. We cannot force the Promised Isaac into fulfilment. **The Visitation of the Lord God will bring that time of fulfilment to us (Jeremiah 29:10).** Our part is to make ourselves ready and available to receive *the Revival Mandate of His Word*. And we know that God is not slack concerning His planned Mandate and Promise.

I prophesy, in the Name of Jesus Christ, and proclaim by the Power of the Spirit, *the Words of Adonai*, "Sarah (My Church) shall conceive, and in due time, give birth to the promised Isaac (the magnificent Glory Move) which I have appointed. I, the Lord, have marked the place and time. My Spirit shall move mightily upon you, My children, and My Glory shall be seen in you." Then shall we say to those near and far, "Arise and shine, for your Light has come and the 'Glory (the Kavod)' of the Lord God has risen upon you (Isaiah 60:1–2)."

Prayer:
Heavenly Father, we submit to Your Word. Let Your Glory rest upon us at the appointed time. In Jesus' Name, Amen...

May You Be Filled With Exceeding Joy & Laughter On the Great Awakening Day!

The Ordained Birth of the Great Awakening is at Hand   CHAPTER 6

'Papua New Guinea

— *out of you shall come the Great Revival Fire'*

CHAPTER 7

PROPHECY: the Great Move of God Will Start in Papua New Guinea

When a nation is Baptised in Fire, then shall come a spilling over that cannot be contained.
PNG! Out of you shall come the Great Move of God.

*I*t's time to submit to you what I see in the Spirit. This prophecy is carrying great weight, which I believe will come to pass *at His Appointed Time*. The time of fulfilment is fast approaching, and I am compelled by the Spirit to speak to the Church about her *posture and positioning for the Glory*. Saints, it will be *the shaking of the nations*.

Please pardon my directness. I have no intention to be presumptuous nor am I boastful concerning the Heart of God, because these are His things—for us. I want to begin by speaking directly to your hearts... Such a grandiose thing as the Great Move must in all its fullness remain as a God-thing—*coming from God* and not from man. I understand that there are many other prophecies about the Move of God and where it should begin, and I have carefully weighed each of those claims. I encourage you to consider each prophecy on its merit, with prayerful consideration of its alignment with biblical revelation. Even as I submit what I believe is of the Lord, I leave room for you to judge, and that is the right thing to do. I do ask you, with all sincerity, that you consider what the Spirit has laid upon me as *a burden*.

Which leads me to the question, "Where is God's intended Glory-Move going to start from?"... That's a subject of great interest to me. I first heard about this prophecy in 1999. I know of many ministers who have spoken of this coming Glory, and they have expressed their desire to see its fulfilment. I personally hadn't received any *specific* Words from the Lord concerning the Great Awakening until I had my encounter with the Spirit of God. On the 26th of January 2022, during our usual Wednesday night fellowship meeting. This meeting was nothing out of the ordinary for us, but as we worshipped the Lord, the place was filled with God's Presence, the prophetic began to flow, and the Word of the Lord came upon me. It was prophecy of a different kind that I was used to, so tangible, and heavy with the Power of the Spirit—I would hazard a guess that it was *the highest level of Prophecy* (a topic I may have to write in another book). Heightened understanding came to me when the Lord spoke, and there He revealed His Plans to me (Amos 3:7–8).

The revelation that I received was that the Great Revival Mandate is to begin at a particular geographical location of His choosing. I gained additional insight that same night about the *preparatory Moves of the Spirit*, which I have talked about in this book.

Before I continue, I must lay a *foundational Truth* for you concerning this prophecy... Hear me: Heaven has already addressed the matter. and it has come from the Lord. The *time*, *place, and vessels have been chosen and are fully known to Him.* This is His sovereign will and intent for us. Therefore, you must decide—will you receive it in faith and respond in obedience, or will you let it pass you by? Like Habakkuk, we must stand watch, with our hearts ready to receive this Great Move of the Spirit:

> "I will stand upon my watch, and set me upon the tower, and will watch to see what He will say unto me, and what I shall answer when I am reproved. And the LORD answered me, and said, 'Write the vision, and make it plain upon tables, that **he may run that readeth it. For the vision is yet for an appointed time, but at the end it shall speak, and not lie:** though it tarry, wait for it; because it will surely come, it will not tarry'... For the earth shall be filled with the knowledge of the Glory of the LORD, as the waters cover the sea. (Habakkuk 2:1–3,14)"

As God's messenger, I have proclaimed to you that which I have *seen and heard*. I know that *the hour of fulfilment* is fast approaching us. Thus, I have reflected deeply on the message, like the prophet Amos did, when he said,

> "Can two walk together, except they be agreed?... Surely the Lord GOD will do nothing, but **He revealeth His Secret unto His servants the prophets.** The lion hath roared, who will not fear? **The Lord GOD hath SPOKEN, who can but prophesy?** (Amos 3:3, 7–8)."

PART 4   *The Birth of the Great Move (Prophetic Foundations)*

Here is where I answer the question, "Where will the Greatest (Glory) Awakening begin?" The answer that I have received is... Papua New Guinea (PNG). Without further ado, here's the Prophecy for you to consider:

" THIS IS THE WAY THE LORD WANTS IT.
PAPUA NEW GUINEA, OUT OF YOU SHALL COME THE GREAT REVIVAL

Listen. **It's the way the Lord wants it... It's the way the Lord wants it... It's the way the Lord wants it.**

PNG, out of you shall come THE GREAT REVIVAL. Out of you shall come THE GREAT MOVE...Out of you shall come THE GREAT MOVE.

When a nation is baptised in Fire, then shall come a spilling over that shall not be contained. Then shall come a spilling that shall overflow and break past its borders. Then shall come the spilling over that shall overtake and run over. Then shall come the spilling, says the LORD.

(As I proclaimed the prophetic Word of the Lord, the Spirit showed me a Vision of the Great Revival like mighty waters rising and how it would rise out of the land of PNG; from the Heart of PNG and fall upon Australia with a great impact)

Oh, PNG, stretch your hands.

AUSTRALIA: ELEVATE! says the Lord. ELEVATE! and come away from the flesh and the soulish man, AUSTRALIA.

TORRES STRAIT ISLANDS, this is His Will. THIS IS HIS WILL. TORRES STRAIT, nothing is hard for God. And the idol culture over you is broken, and you are released from that bondage in the Name of Jesus. For I shall speak to you with My love songs, says the LORD. Torres Strait, I shall speak to you with Words of kindness, and of goodness and gentleness…I shall speak to you.

For in an hour that you do not expect, shall I come. And you shall be called "Holiness of the Lord!" Pray and Yield TORRES STRAIT. Don't you KNOW GOD'S PLAN? And did you not SEE and UNDERSTAND it? Or are you afraid of God's PLAN? If you are, then step aside and let Him show you. For the PLAN OF GOD will come to pass—it shall come to pass in the Name of Jesus. God is not going to pass you by, TORRES STRAIT ISLANDS. God is not going to pass you by anymore. For the Island nations are waiting for you, TORRES STRAIT ISLANDS.

Then shall AUSTRALIA see the Spirit of God. And AUSTRALIA shall know the Name of the LORD GOD. At that time, the nations will drink in Australia first. That is, those who have migrated to Australia, who come from different nations… They will drink the GREAT CUP OF GOD'S MIGHTY MOVE given to Australia. Then, Torres Strait Islanders, you shall go way south to the end of Australia and west. Torres Strait Island… You shall catch the Fire from PNG. (Amen and Amen)."

What stood out to me by the Holy Spirit were the opening words of the prophecy. I felt the Holy Ghost emphasise the words with a burdened utterance. "Listen… **This is the way the Lord wants it.**" The Lord placed great emphasis on those Words and made me see that He is very much invested in and committed to *the Plan* to release His Glory upon the Earth. The Spirit emphasised that He is going to ignite it in a *specific place*, through a *specific vessel (and vessels)*, and at *an appointed time*. *The place*, *the vessel* and *the time* are all firmly established in His Divine Plan and cannot be altered, nor disputed. God has already chosen.

As I write these words, the passage of Jeremiah 29:10 comes to mind, where the Lord is saying, "...I will visit you, and perform My good Word toward you, in causing you to return to THIS PLACE." Yes, those Words were for Israel at that time. Even now, the greater intent behind those Words is for us in this very hour. For He will visit us at the appointed time, and His Glory shall be seen upon us and in us... HE SHALL BE SEEN. If you believe this, say "Amen!"

Let's pause for a moment to pray:
Oh, Spirit of God, come upon us with great Power. Fill our hearts with Your Presence. Lift our heads from the graves of discouragement and cause us to abide in pleasant places of Your Presence. Come, Lord Jesus, come, and let Your Glory be seen upon us and in us. Hallelujah! In Your Name, Amen...

Waves of His Glory and Divine Assignments

Glory Encounters are going to be released like great tides of the waves of the sea. What flows from our *Times of Refreshing in the Holy Ghost* becomes in us, Living Waters gushing forth to reach many (John 7:38). As the waves of the sea billow from one to another and surge into a powerful momentum, so will God's Chosen Ones be positioned to *catch the Fire* and carry it to wherever the Spirit leads them. Their obedience to the Holy Spirit will cause the momentum of the Wave of His Fire to increase rapidly and go forth to the nations.

And if you haven't yet seen it, you're going to see a *continuous current of encounters* until they burst forth into an *overflow!* I call it "The Great Gushing of God." That is the Fire that rests upon us— the gushing of His Glory, Hallelujah! That is why I said that *the preliminary Fires* carry great depth and significance in God. The Spirit is ministering deeper things to us, *preparing our hearts to receive the greater Glory.* And I am encouraged, for *the nearness of the Spirit* is continuing to do a mighty work in us.

Psalms 40:5

Many, O LORD my God, are Thy wonderful works which Thou hast done, and Thy thoughts which are to us-ward: they cannot be reckoned up in order unto Thee: if I would declare and speak of them, they are more than can be numbered.

Joy fills my heart as I look to the *Dawn of His Rising* because I know that *the build-up* from the *preparatory Moves* will lead to the Great Gushing Day of the Spirit.

Friends, *Glory Encounters release Divine Assignments.* In the preparatory stage, we will see *Tides* of His Glory overflowing upon us with *Revival Assignments.* Because the Glory that manifests flows with intent. That is the way God has intended it. One Revival assignment will lead to another, until the mighty tide of His Revival Fire breaks forth with great intensity.

> **REVIVAL TRUTH:**
> " Glory Encounters release Divine Assignments.

The Road to Fulfilment

It is due time. The Light shining on the road to fulfilment is getting brighter as *the Day* draws near. And God is already releasing the initial showers of the *Latter Rain*... As we speak, *Preparatory Moves* are being received everywhere on the Earth, and God is already doing a mighty work in the midst of His people. A Spirit-led *priming or preparation* is in progress. This initial work is to prepare the hearts for the *Greater Glory*.

With that in mind, many have already been stirred in the Spirit to say to you, "I have come with a Word from the Lord." I encourage you not to be fearful or cynical concerning this holy thing. For **Holy Conversations flow from Holy Grounds.** I encourage you to grab hold, with faith, every blessing that flows from these holy moments ordained to us—and do it *early*. It is the Lord's *good intent for you* (Jeremiah 29:10–11). Know that you are playing your part in the build-up process, and in the Church, welcoming the drawing near of *the Day of the Great Awakening*.

In light of this, we must make our hearts ready to receive Him. It starts with each of us obeying the Holy Spirit in every little and big Revival Assignment given to us. Responding with partial obedience is failing to obey correctly. And if we really want to receive the abundance of His Presence, we must be *broken and free* from any earthly hindrances so that we can accommodate *the Word of Glory*. We must set aside our differences, including disagreements, cynicism or assumptions of others, and our skewed (fleshly) views of the Move of God. It's time for us to *unite* and *host* the Holy Spirit with one heart. We can only achieve this with a spirit of Grace—with tender hearts—in a spirit of reconciliation, and with a true desire for unity. Know that you are doing this for your Church family, your community, your city, your region, and your nation.

"Heaven values your alignment to every God Assignment placed upon you.

The Spillover from PNG to Australia, & then to the Nations

Additional notes:

I now want to tie in an important thought. There are sections in my previous book, Chosen to Carry the Glory— Carry the Fire of Jesus, ...Particularly in Chapter 5—*The Glory Cloud Encounter and Australia*,[8] that connect to the Prophecy about PNG, Torres Strait Islands and Australia. The PNG Prophecy declares that it will start with PNG and that Papua New Guinea will be *the Birthplace* of the Great Move of God. Then, from PNG, the Fire will spill over to Australia (The ordained *Launching Platform* to the nations).

My current thoughts on it are that the effects of this mighty outpouring will be felt throughout the world. The spillover from PNG will come upon the Torres Strait Island people in a mighty way. Most Torres Strait Islanders live in the northern part of Queensland, Australia, mainly in Cairns City. This is one of the places where the spillover from PNG first becomes evident in Australia. While this is happening, a Revival Wave will also hit the heart of Australia and the East Coast of Australia. The impact will be so tremendous and is going to shake Australia with *great Heavenly Force*. It will change the very culture of the nation to a *God Culture*.

And because Australia is a multi-cultural nation, it is easy to see here how the nations of the Earth will begin to drink of the Outpouring of the Spirit. That's when the Prophecy concerning

Australia truly begins. Australia will then become *The Platform — the Launching Pad* from which the Move of God will go forth and reach the nations.

Saints, God's Revival Mandate is *in order*, and what must follow will follow correctly, according to *God's intent*. For the zeal of the Lord will perform this.

I encourage you, by the Holy Spirit, to first consider the prophecy in light of what is already happening in the Church (1 Corinthians 14:29), and then thoroughly soak up *the PNG — Australia — Nations* Prophecy into your spirit and be ready to receive *the Great Wave of His Glory.*

May the Glory of the Great Awakening Rise Upon
You At the Break of Dawn!

ENDNOTE:

8. (Sabadi, N.M.T, 2023. Chapter 5 The Glory Cloud & Australia, *Chosen to Carry the Glory — Carry the Fire of Jesus*, Norman Sabadi Publishing, Rockhampton, Queensland, Australia pp.17).

CHAPTER 7

PART 4   *The Birth of the Great Move (Prophetic Foundations)*

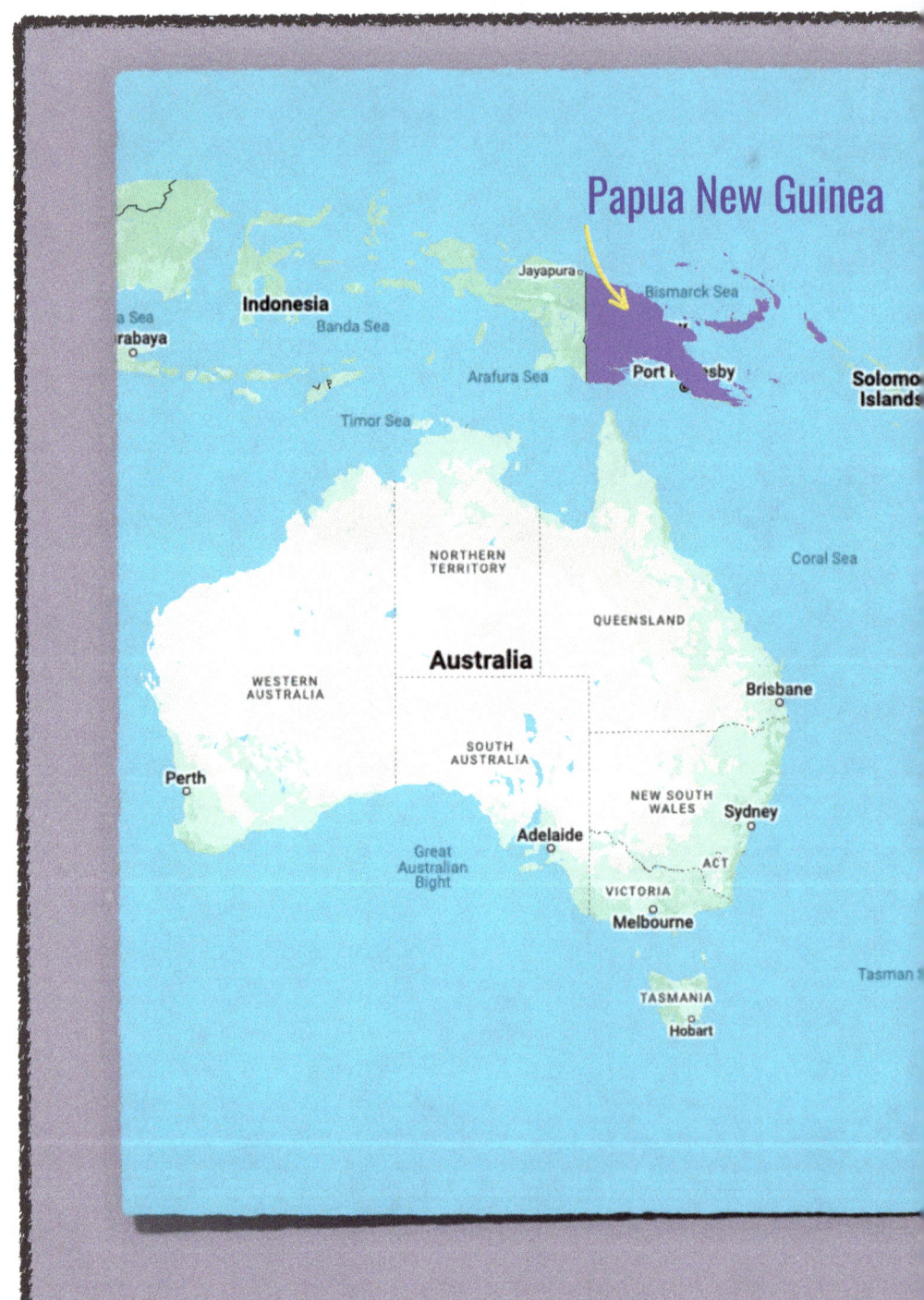

Map of Papua New Guinea, Australia (Oceania Region)

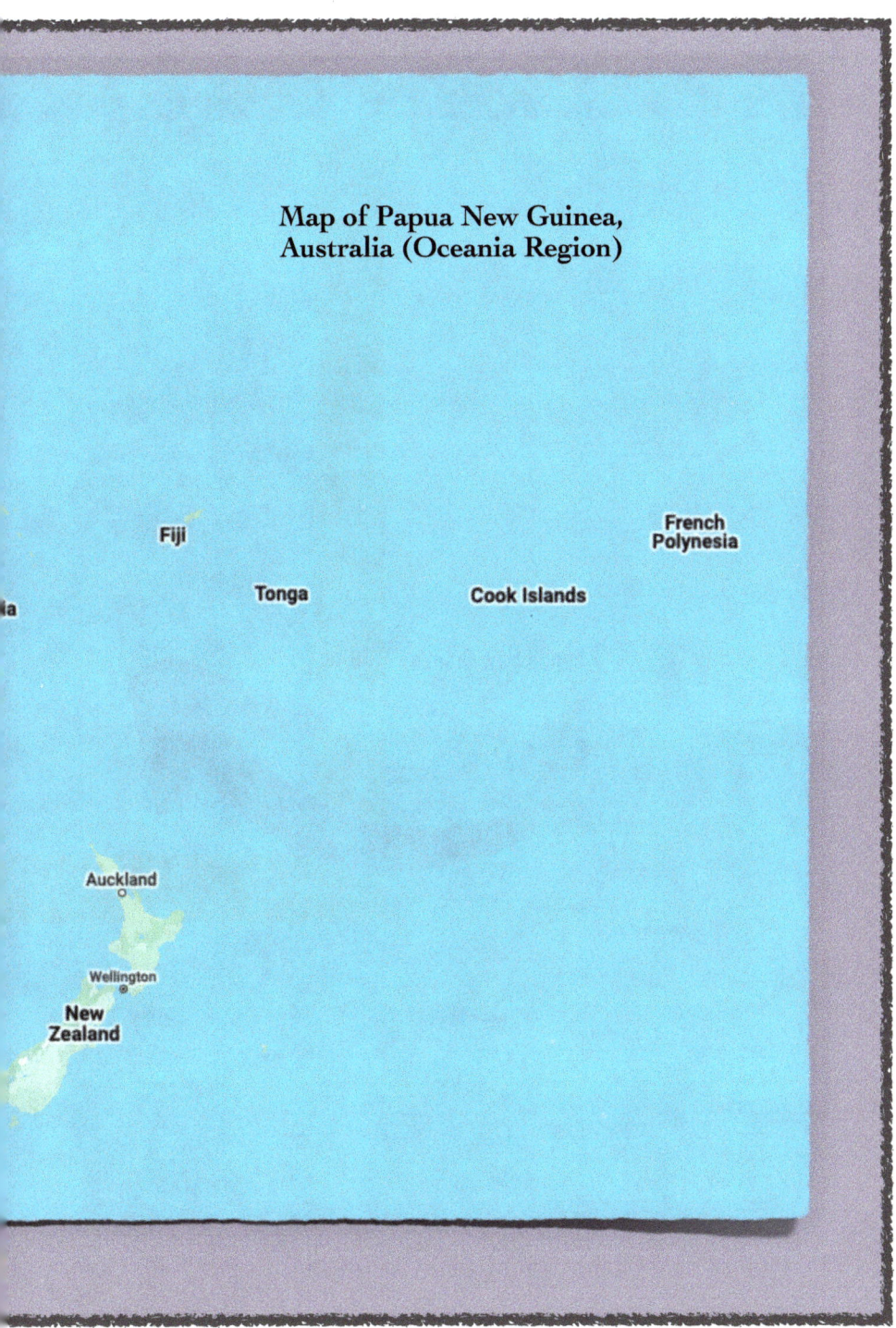

PART 4   *The Birth of the Great Move (Prophetic Foundations)*

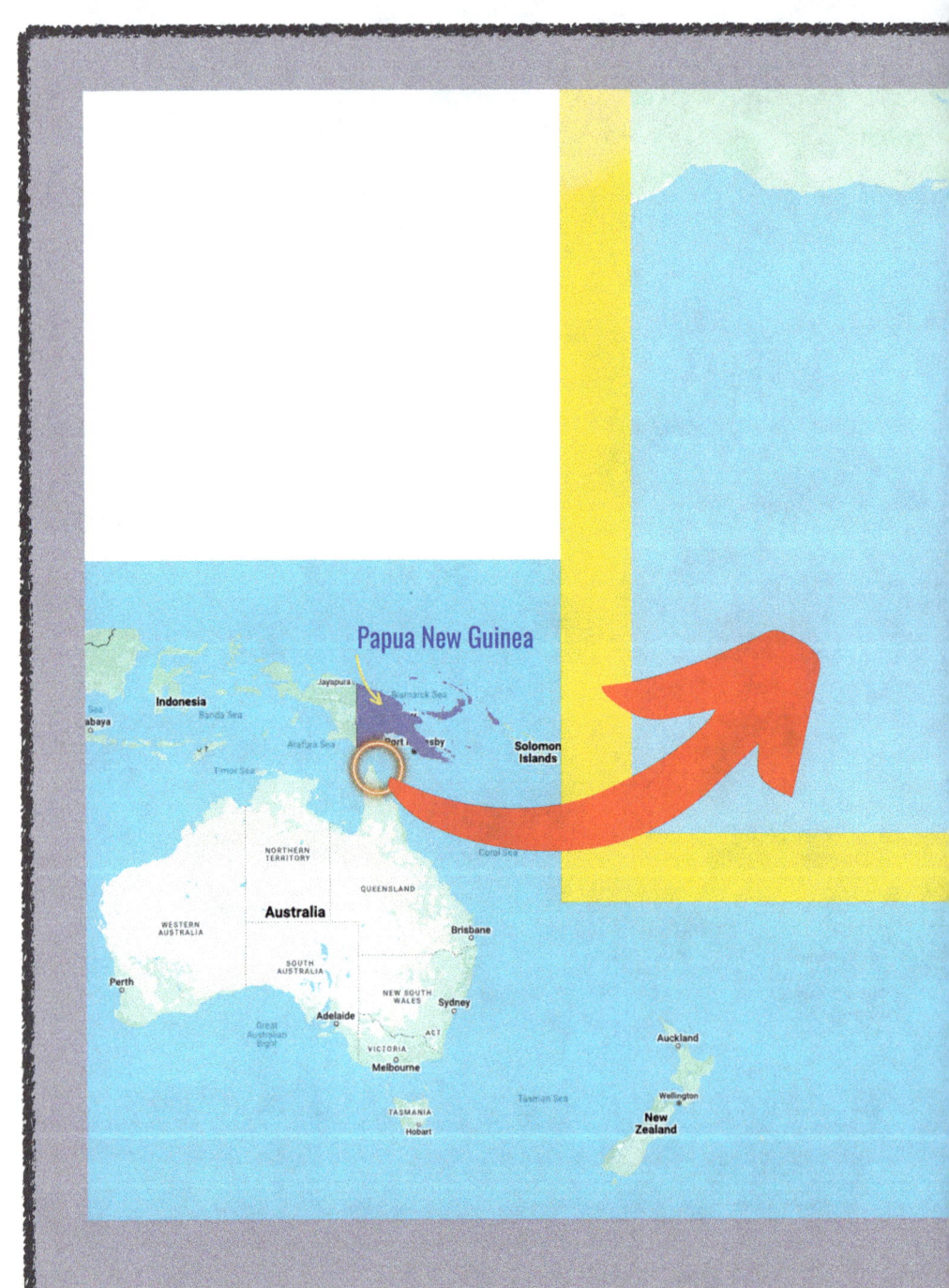

PROPHECY: *The Great Move of God Will Start In Papua New Guinea* CHAPTER 7

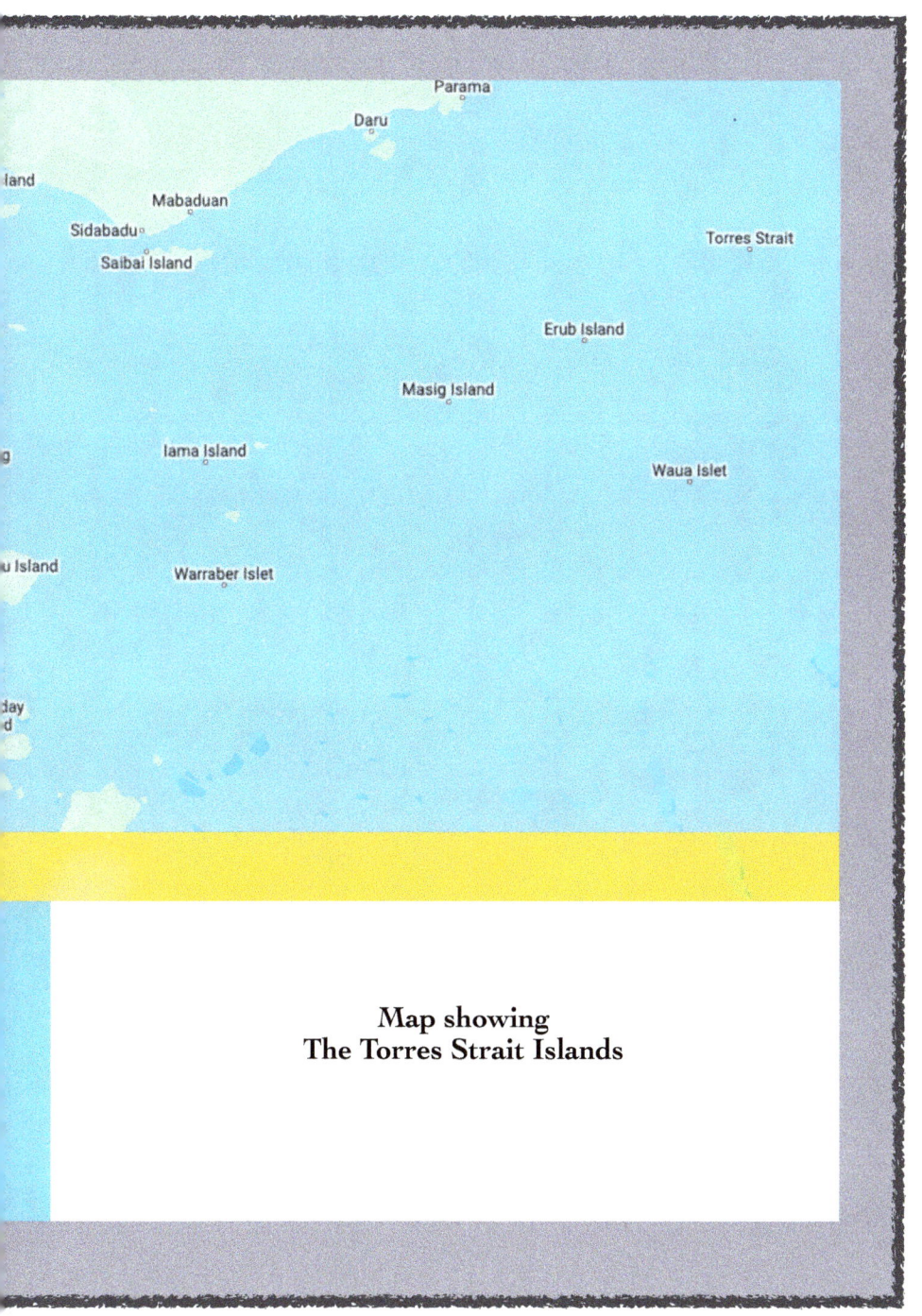

**Map showing
The Torres Strait Islands**

Part 5 – God's Chosen Leader – The Revivalist

God says, "I have appointed Me a LEADER and My Revival, it will enter the Churches."

Wednesday 20th April 2022

CHAPTER 8

Sheep With No Shepherd

They have no shepherd to lead them.

Matthew 9:36–38

But when He saw the multitudes, He was moved with compassion on them, because they fainted, and were scattered abroad, **as sheep having no shepherd.** Then saith He unto His disciples, The harvest truly is plenteous, but the labourers are few; **Pray ye therefore the Lord of the harvest, that He will send forth labourers into his harvest.**

A great chasm stands between those who have opened their hearts to carry, lead, and serve the Move of God, and those who, from a distance, attempt to explain the Revival Fire they have not yet fully entered. This great divide will be bridged, as God's Spirit moves mightily to unite His People.

The Church needs fathers and mothers of the Move who are carrying a tangible Revival Anointing to lead the way. Yet this is easier said than done, for many leaders still hold fast to *the tap of Revival*. I have observed how so many have taken on an obstinate posture and turned away from the *Burning* of His Word. As a result, they have distanced themselves from the Great Revival Fire—whether they know this or not. Despite this, the Lord has anointed His Revivalists with a sacred *Commission and Mantle*—to disciple and lead the Church into the Blessed Revival Fire.

> **"Revival leadership is the answer for Revival.**

Recently, I was at a particular meeting—not as a speaker, but among a gathering of believers who had come together to worship God and receive His Word. As I prayed quietly, the Holy Spirit spoke to me and said, "Look at them. They have *no Shepherd* to lead them." I opened my eyes, scanned the room, and in that moment of epiphany, I understood the heart of God's message. A knowing flooded my spirit, and revelation from the Lord was instantly downloaded within me. Immediately, I felt His Heart for the people —overflowing with care and compassion for His Church.

The next thing He showed me was a "Stirring"—I cannot think of any other word to describe it. I felt the Spirit captivate my heart as I beheld *the veil lifted from this mystery*. I saw that although there were leaders in the room—the likes of pastors, elders, and prophets —they were not the ones He was looking at. His gaze was very much like when He picked David, and caused the prophet Samuel to see what He saw in David (1 Samuel 16:6–13). This insight was deeply compelling in that it was not only to do with a heart matter, but had everything to do with God's *Revival Anointing and the Mandate—God was being specific on the matter*. The person He was looking for had to be one mantled with His Glory Mandate. God was talking about a more significant and distinct person—*His appointed Revivalist.* This chosen Fire Carrier will lead God's people and teach them how to enter into the Glory of His Revival Fire.

> **REVIVAL TRUTH:**
> " God's chosen Fire Carrier will lead God's people and teach them how to enter into the Glory of the Revival Fire.

God was looking for one who knew His Heart and would lead His people along the glorious path toward *the blessing of hosting His Glory.*

I looked at the people around me: the sheep of God's pasture. I noticed their enthusiasm and commitment—you couldn't fault that. I saw the zeal and passion they had for God, but *they didn't know how to be aware of Him. They didn't know how to be a people of His Abiding Glory.* Their lack of awareness was causing this error. They were sheep without a *Chosen Shepherd* (an Anointed One—a Revivalist). They had no *Revival-Shepherd* to lead them to the *Promised Land of God's magnificent Revival Fire.* What was eye-opening and particularly intriguing was that they had their overseeing pastor with them in the room, but he wasn't a *Revivalist* —God's eyes were not on Him. Right there and then, it was plain before me that **the Mantle of the Revivalist is a most distinctive Mantle with a unique realm of operation.** The Power of this Mantle separates him from all the other ministers. Only a Glory Carrier can lead the sheep and show them how to host the Presence of God. The Lord wanted His Revivalist to show them *the pathway to the Promise.*

If you study Revival history—from Moses to the Upper Room, and from the Upper Room to Azusa Street, up until now—you will see this unchanging Truth. Every Move requires a *Catalyst (a Fire Starter)*, and every Move is sustained by their *appointed Catalyst—the Revivalist—the Glory Carrier.* That individual, when used by God, goes from being used to start the Move of God to carrying, leading and serving the purpose of the Move. Only a chosen vessel, carrying *the Mandated Assignment,* is used by the Lord to release the Move of God. The Mandate to release the Move is first *conceived* in him and then remains upon him as a BURDEN from the Lord, until it is released at *the appointed time.*

> **REVIVAL TRUTH:**
>
> **" Every Move of God requires a Catalyst (a Fire Starter), every Move is sustained by their appointed Catalyst.**

A relevant thought:
Moves don't die out... Their Fires continue burning in those who were impacted by them. The Fire of God burns in them as a *living experience.* Adding to that, the Lord will continue to pour out His Spirit upon as many as have made themselves available to *catch the Fire.*

The Fire upon this chosen Revivalist, carries with it God's powerful Mandate, and it will cause him to raise an army of Fire Carriers, or sons and daughters of the Move—*these are Fire-carrying individuals who get ignited by the Fire flowing from the Catalyst.* This is how the Great Awakening Fire is going to be received and spread.

> **"God will use a 'Chosen One—a Witness of the Fire' to start and release the mighty Revival Fire.**

I could see how the Spirit wanted the sheep to have His Fire, and was looking for *His Fire Carrier* and calling him to take his place amongst them. (This Chosen Burning One) His defining *hallmark* is the Fire of the Word burning deep within His Spirit. This goes beyond just revelation knowledge. It becomes in him a torrent of Heavenly Power flowing through his being. This is that *Word of Power* that is resting upon the Glory Carrier.

I was quite moved as I beheld this unfolding revelation. This Heavenly insight came with a *great burden*. I felt God's cry and I wanted to cry with Him. I felt His desire for His people and I wanted it for them too. I wondered what could I do to help?

I could feel the stirring of God within me. I knew what the people needed. I knew that they needed the Glory of His Abiding Word in their midst, and they needed *their appointed Word-carrying leader* to do this. They needed someone of this calibre (A Glory Carrier), whose merits were ordained and approved by God. Someone *clothed with a Revival Mantle—a Burning One*. This specially chosen leader is mandated by the Fire resting on him to lead God's people, garbed with the *kingly and priestly Anointing of Christ*. Only God by His Authority can assign this leader to the sheep (note the bolded words).

Isaiah 55:3–4

…Behold, I have given him for a witness to the people, a leader and commander to the people.

May the Lord Grant You His Revivalist, to Lead You Into the Day of His Great Awakening!

"I shall send you to be in their midst and you shall speak for Me. For you shall release My Revival Fire upon them—My Messenger of Discipline... Teach them My Posture and First Love."

CHAPTER 9

Leader of the Great Revival

Lead us there to the Great Waters of God's Glory.

As noted in the previous chapter, Revival comes through God's Revivalist. *The Command for Revival* requires a mighty *Revival Mantle*... That Mantle rests upon the Glory Carrier. This is the way the Lord has ordained it. *This Burning One will lead the Great Revival Mandate.*

The Holy Spirit Will Lead the Move Through His Revivalist

The Holy Ghost will lead the Move through *His Revivalist*. The *Revivalist is marked by God's Revival Anointing*. This chosen individual will stand up to proclaim God's Word at the appointed time. The Church will not be able to receive the Revival Blessing until the Church first receives God's appointed *Word Carrier* and

Mantle Wearer. Jesus knew what was coming ahead for the Church and it was His intent for the Holy Spirit to be given to us, not only as our Comforter, but as our *Leader and Commander.* It is of great importance that you understand this because if you do, you will recognise and receive *the Revival Blessing.* The truth is, you cannot claim apostolic leadership without *Holy Spirit leadership.*[2]

That being said, there are two specific *classes of vessels* who will receive a mandate:

> **REVIVAL TRUTH:**
>
> " You cannot claim apostolic leadership without Holy Spirit leadership

- The Leader and Fire Starter (the Catalyst, Carrier and Servant) of the Great Revival, and
- The Chosen Revival Leaders, Fire Carriers (who will carry the Fire to their Churches, to their nation, to their people, cities and towns, and to their families.

Again, this is a God-thing. It is a *holy ground discussion.* Its selection is of the Lord and not of man. It was the Lord who made all these things known to me with the intent that I be a faithful steward and publish (or make known) His Plans for the Body of Christ (Galatians 1:12). In the same year, in which I received the 'PNG Prophecy,' the Lord continued speaking to me about His specific chosen leader, His chosen leaders for the preliminary Moves, and also for the coming Great Move. I would like to share these prophecies with you.

> **REVIVAL TRUTH:**
> " The responsibility of releasing the Move will come through *God's Chosen* Revivalist.

Prophecy—I Have Appointed A Leader to Lead My People

The following prophecies were received in Cairns City, Australia, in April and May 2022. These prophecies speak directly to the Body of Christ concerning *the Lord's Revival Initiative and Mandate*.

My prayer is that as you read the prophecies, you will weigh them in your heart and consider these *revelational insights* (2 Timothy 3:16–17) and be willing to adjust, if necessary, to what the Spirit is saying to the Churches. For we are called to be a holy nation before Him (1 Peter 2:9).

Prophecy - Wed 20 Apr 2022

The Move of God will not come in the way that many people have expected it—not in the way that the Churches have anticipated it. And God is going to continue to repeat this over and over in our ears so that we can understand that it's not going to come in the way that we have perceived it or in the way that we have intended it. "**But it is already here…**" says the Lord.

(Note: the bolded part speaks about *the preparatory Move* of God that is currently happening in the Church.)

The Lord has appointed His leaders. He also has appointed the LEADER that will continue with it. This leader will become vocal. He will begin to sense the direction of God in different areas. And He will begin to host meetings—one meeting after another... One meeting will follow the other which will follow the other. And He will learn to avoid that which is bad and stick to that which is good. For he will discern what is not of God, and stick to what is good.

God says, "I have appointed a LEADER to lead My people. And My Revival Fire will enter the Churches." At the time that He appoints—one Church after the other, it shall begin to pour and enter the Churches. "For I have appointed a leader to lead My people," says the Lord.

An Anointing of worship will pour upon (us), Cairns. A sweet aroma shall come. At the place where I have appointed, with the *appointed Leader* which I have spoken of. Him, shall the LORD use. There shall be an aroma of worship.

"The false prophets speak not My Words," says the Lord. "For the desire of their own hearts has exposed them. And I will expose them more. I will expose the hidden works of darkness, even of Jezebel."

Prophecy - Sun 10 April 2022

...*He is going to resurrect the pastors. And there's going to be life again in the meetings and there's going to be a lot of evening services.*

Prophecy - Wed 13 Apr 2022

It is a Revival—but *not* in the way the pastors have perceived it. It is a Move—ordained, not ordained by man, but God. It will not come in the way that they have chosen—with their own preferences and their selected ministers. Not even at their own time. But the MOVE will come in a way that they did not expect. In fact, they would easily judge this one and think nothing about it.

But the Spirit says, "My VANAGI[9] (My *Canoe*) is about to set sail. And no one is going to stop it. For the people shall see My Glory and it shall rise upon this land. They shall see My Goodness and My Glory. And I will be the '*healing*' to My people—the Sun of righteousness with healing in My wings. They shall call Me their Lord and I will be their God. This is the remnant which I have Chosen. They will hear My Voice and they will come to Me and I will heal their land. *For My Vanagi (Canoe) is about to set sail*"... This is the Word of the Lord declared to us.

Prophecy - Fri 27 May 2022
The Tide and Canoes Explained.

The Tide is coming in and the Canoes are set to sail. (They need leadership—*Holy Ghost leadership that will bring them into their Blessing*). The Tide—is the Revival Fire of the Holy Ghost. The Canoes—are the chosen remnant of ministers who will rise as *Carriers* of the Revival Fire to release upon the land (*in one Spirit of Revival*).

Having reflected on the prophecies and all that concerns the preliminary Moves and the coming Great Glory, I must address an important issue regarding our *prayers for Revival*. First, I want to acknowledge you—each one of you—who has diligently cried out to the Lord for Revival. But hear me now: when you enter your next prayer meeting, ask yourself this question:

"Do you know what you are praying for?

I submit this Revival Truth to you: don't just pray for Revival, **pray for the Revivalist—the one appointed to bring the Move of God to you.** That person is either already in your Church and among you, or he will be sent to you. Pray that your heart will be open and ready to receive God's Revivalist. Pray that God will give you discernment and understanding and cause your hearts to incline to His Will for you. And lastly, pray also that you will be used by God. The scriptural foundation for this Truth is in Luke 10, when Jesus appointed and sent out seventy disciples.

Luke 10:2
Therefore said He (Jesus) unto them, The harvest truly is great, but the labourers are few: pray ye therefore the Lord of the harvest, that **He would send forth labourers** into His harvest.

Being aware of this, I tell you boldly: the quickest path to receiving the Blessed Move is for Church leaders to open their hearts to receive Revival Fire leaders—whether they be part of the Church's leadership team or not. The Mantle for Revival is already in our midst. The Chosen Revivalist stands ready. Will you let the Move of God break through among you, or will you hold back? Do not limit God with protocol; receive the one He sends you.

"The responsibility of releasing the Move rests as a Mantle on the shoulders of God's Chosen Revivalist.

May You Gladly Receive the Messenger of Good Tidings—God's Chosen Revivalist!

ENDNOTE:

9. Vanagi is a Motuan word, meaning canoe. Motu is the language spoken by the Motuan Group of Villages along the Southern Coast of Papua New Guinea.

When it comes to Revival Leadership God picks His own and He trains His own.

CHAPTER 10

Marked With Fire

'Chosen to Carry the Glory—Carry the Fire of Jesus.'

The coming Great Outpouring will be ushered in by *disciplined Revival Leaders* who walk in the Heart and Mind of God. And hear this: if you want to be used by the Holy Spirit to carry His Fire, you must first be MARKED. **God's Baptism of Fire must come upon you, and mark you for His purpose before you can lead God's people.** For it is that Fire—burning so intensely within you—that will go with you to lead God's people into His Glory.

> **REVIVAL TRUTH:**
> " A Baptism of Fire must first mark you before you can lead God's people.

In my reflections about this highly esteemed call to be a *Revivalist*, I was prompted by the Spirit to look at the story of one of

Israel's great generals, and a powerful leader of God's people: *Joshua*. He was chosen by the Lord to lead the Israelites into the Promised Land. And a special *Anointing marked his life.*

> **REVIVAL TRUTH:**
>
> " A disciple of the Fire of God must serve under a mentor who carries the Fire of God.

Joshua was Moses's minister and devoted servant, walking closely with him and serving with unwavering faithfulness. Like his spiritual father, he walked uniquely before the Lord. God recognised and declared that he had the right spirit to be Israel's next leader (Numbers 27:15–23). When the time came for Moses to depart, the responsibility to lead the nation needed to rest upon a *new leader*. Astoundingly, it was the antecedent process, already in place. The all-knowing God was very much aware of this upcoming appointment right from the time Israel had departed Egypt to embark on their journey to the Promised Land. God knew well that He needed to raise one like Moses who would later become the next leader of His people. And He already knew Joshua was the right person. He gave Joshua a certain degree of access to His Presence (Exodus 33:9-11) because that level of access was important. Its purpose was to expose Joshua to the Glory Cloud and to the Heart and Mind of God. In much the same way, God has worked to mould and prepare His Revival Leaders.

The important aspects of this *Revival training* include:
- Mentoring from a Revival Leader,
- Walking in submission to God and to His Chosen Revival Leader (But please understand that this is a *submission out of love and respect*; not out of duty and obligation. Such a submission

comes naturally and it must be from our hearts, not forced upon us),
- Exposure to the Presence and Voice of God,
- Obedience to the Voice of God,
- Undergoing seasons of moulding and preparation for God's use,
- Embracing Revival Truths, and
- Being marked with Fire.

Stemming from this Revival training, the type of leader that God wants will have the *right spirit*. Joshua was an example of this. He:
- *instinctively* followed the Voice of God,
- *reverently* followed the Voice of God,
- *willingly* followed the Voice of God, and
- *confidently* followed the Voice of God.

God ensured that Joshua would be discipled by Moses (The Revivalist). In a sovereign way, beyond man's comprehension, God works supernaturally to prepare a vessel of His choosing and marks them with His Power. I marvel at the thought that *Glory* has looked down from Heaven and has already set His eyes on one, saying, "Unto this man will I look. To him that trembles at My Word (Isaiah 66:2)."...*God picks His own and He trains His own*.

> ## REVIVAL TRUTH:
> " *The Encounter* that separates and sanctifies, is the encounter that comes to mark God's Revivalists.

Studying the aspects of this God-ordained, God-designed Revival training, we see that Joshua was exposed to conversations that Moses had with the Lord. If you want to carry the Revival Fire, you must first be *exposed continuously* to the Power of the Word, and you must want to *be discipled* by the Fire Carrier. This is the pattern for Revival training established by God. *A disciple of the Fire of God must serve under a mentor who carries the Fire.*

On a related note:
The role of a spiritual father is not only to lead God's people but to teach them how to walk with God. He mentors them so they don't need to solely depend on him. The mission of the leader is to show the sheep how to pursue God for themselves and then release them. For them to do this correctly, their appointed mentor has to be *their example*. That's how Revival Leadership works.

While on this thought, we must be careful not to make ourselves His Revivalists according to our own standards or by humanly stirred efforts. *It is the Fire of God that picks the vessel.* Our part to play is to seek, submit and surrender to God, and His part is to *mark us with His Fire.*

> **REVIVAL TRUTH:**
> "You cannot inherit Revival unless there is a Fire Starter and a Mentor of Revival. You cannot enter God's Move unless He assigns to you His appointed Revival Leader.

So, just as Joshua was a man whose heart pursued God, so also is the Revivalist. *The Revival Fire will pick a man whose heart is after God's Heart.* That's why the Revivalist is different. Many want to pursue God, but only a few pursue *what He desires.*

A Divine Marking separated Joshua to be *the Leader of God's Mandate.* A specific endowment began to intensify upon him as he, too, was continuously exposed to the Voice and Glory of God. What a wonderful inheritance of encounters bestowed upon Joshua. This *continuous stream of encounters* left a life-changing imprint on him, stirring his heart to pursue God even more. This attitude alone separated him from the rest of Israel's captains and elders. And as soon as the *Charge of God* was placed upon him, *the Anointing to lead God's people was also with him.*

> **REVIVAL TRUTH:**
>
> " The Fire will be *Ignited and Spread* by a chosen leader, chosen leaders, and a chosen people.

Now, another trait concerning Joshua was *his obedience to the Voice of God.* Joshua learned to obey the Lord just like his spiritual father, Moses. It was as Paul wrote in 1 Corinthians 11:1 "Be ye followers of me even as I also am of Christ." Joshua was willing to follow the leading of the Holy Spirit and to trust God. This significant trait also became a distinct marking on Joshua's life. Therefore, *anyone who wants to be a Revivalist must first learn to obey the Voice of the Holy Spirit and be fully given to His Counsels.*

Exodus 19:5–8

Now therefore, if ye will OBEY My Voice indeed, and keep My Covenant, then ye shall be a peculiar treasure unto Me above all people: for all the earth is Mine: And ye shall be unto Me a Kingdom of priests, and an holy nation…

Joshua—Postured to be a Revival Leader

We can learn from the criteria God used to choose His leader. The choosing of Joshua was *God-ordained and God-led* (Numbers 27:15–23, Deuteronomy 31:14–15). Joshua had met God's requirements to be the next leader. But what were these requirements? Let's look at the list closely:
- It's a God-initiated selection (Deuteronomy 31:14–15),
- Joshua walked with God as one whose heart was given to God (Numbers 27:8),
- Joshua had a mentor. He encountered God's Presence while serving his father and mentor, Moses. (Exodus 24:13, Exodus 33:11),
- Joshua learned to know God's Voice and obey God Himself (Joshua 1:1-9, Deuteronomy 31:3),
- Joshua was willing to go where God was leading (Numbers 32:12),
- Joshua was a man who pursued the Presence of God (Exodus 24:13, Exodus 33:11), and
- Joshua served, received and continued in the Anointing and the Mandate that his spiritual father carried.

A Chosen Leader & A Chosen Army

I believe God has already picked His Leader of the Great Revival Mandate and His Revival Leaders. God has picked a people after His Heart and has set them apart to receive Divine direction to *carry the nations into Revival.* Hallelujah! For the timing of the Birth of the Great Move is soon upon us, and the Spirit wants to release the fullness of *His Kavod (weighty Glory)* upon us.

Additional Attributes of a Revivalist Leader

In addition to what we have already considered, the following are markings of the type of Revivalist leader God is looking for:

- He trusts in God,
- He is meek before the Lord, and before God's people,
- He is obedient to the Voice of the Spirit,
- He is given to God's *Anointing and Commission,*
- He is also can *identify, recognise and acknowledge* those who carry an Anointing,
- He ensures these individuals have the opportunity to release what they carry. He creates an environment of growth and a place for the saints to encounter God,
- He builds upon the foundation of:
  - Grace and Truth,
  - Encounter and revelation,
  - Prayerfulness and a true worship posture,
  - A teachable and willing heart,
- He mentors leaders, and He affirms the work of new leaders. He faithfully disciples God's people.
- He is a father of the Move of God, and he carries deepness and closeness with God. He has a Christ-like life (he follows and represents Christ correctly) and,
- He carries, leads and serves the Revival Mantle resting upon his life. He serves the purpose and direction of the Holy Spirit —He serves the Revival Mandate.

Prayer:
Oh, Lord of Glory, send Your Glory through Your Chosen Vessels. Send Your Fire Carriers to the people, in Jesus' Name,

Amen…

May the Revival Fire of God Rest Upon You on the Day of the Great Awakening!

CHAPTER 10

Part 6 – The Elijah Mantle: Preparing the Way Again

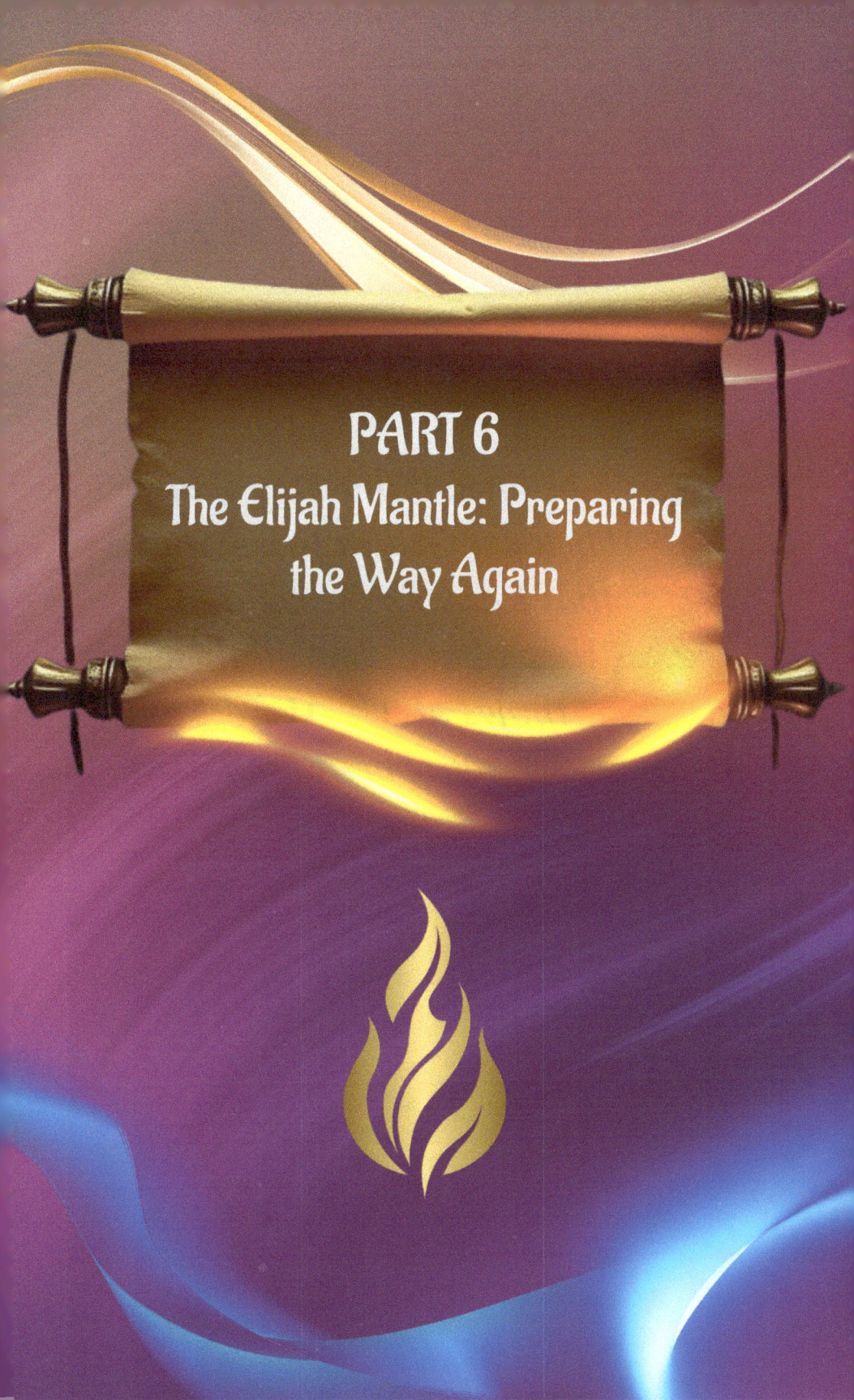

"Let it be known this Day that Thou art God in Israel, and that I am Thy servant, and that I have done all these things at Thy Word."
— Prophet Elijah

CHAPTER 11

The Spirit & Power of Elijah—the Revivalist

*The Great Revival shall come through the Mantle Wearer
who responds to the Word of Glory.*

In the time of the prophet Elijah—about 850 years before Christ—there was a desperate yearning to break free from the oppressive rule of the disobedient and rebellious King Ahab and his wicked queen, Jezebel. Their promotion of the idol worship of Baal across the Kingdom of Israel had brought a curse upon the land, along with every form of wickedness. At that time, the Kingdom of Israel was divided into two kingdoms: Israel to the north—comprising ten of the twelve tribes of Israel—and Judah in the south, made up of the tribes of Judah and Benjamin.

Now Jezebel sought to kill the prophets of the Most High. Many of these servants of God went into hiding for fear of losing their lives. In the thick of this persecution and tribulation, the persistent prayers of the remaining faithful still prevailed. The hearts of the people had grown cold, and a Revival was needed to awaken them.

There was no longer any passion or desire to worship the Lord God. They preferred their idols over *Yahweh*. The altars of idol gods received more adoration and worship, while the Altar of the Lord on Mount Carmel lay in ruins, abandoned and forgotten.

Amidst this spiritual darkness and persecution, one could sense that a stirring was going on in the realm of the spirit. Unfazed by Jezebel's threats, many prophets courageously stood up (in the Power of the Word) to speak against the idolatry that defiled the land. Though their *confrontations* weren't welcomed, the Word of God was stronger in them. A great turning of hearts was drawing near, and the *Zeal of God* was about to break through the darkness and perform His good Word in due season. *Israel's Revival was at the break of dawn.*

The Lord saw what was happening to His people, and a passionate zeal was in His Heart. *The God of the Burning Bush* was postured to birth Revival. To achieve this, God first had to *send a unique Word*. A mighty call would come forth and be heard by one who was forged in the crucible of this tribulation. A chosen one—who was born for Israel's *Revival*. It was time for *the confrontation of hearts*. The Lord initiated His Plan by *sending His Revivalist* to turn the hearts of the disobedient toward righteousness and to cause the hearts of the leaders of the nation to return to Him.

Among the sons of the prophets was one man, a unique firebrand of God, who knew *the Heart* of God and walked in His Ways. A man from the mountains of Gilead (east of the Jordan River), named Elijah (Hebrew: *Eliyahu*, meaning *Yahweh is my God, or my God is Yahweh*). This prophet had the Fire of God's Anointing burning in his bones. A mighty *Revival Anointing* and *ordinance of the Spirit* rested upon him. No doubt, God's intentions were going to be fulfilled through *this chosen vessel*.

Elijah appeared on the scene, and right from the start, there was a *weightiness in the Words* that he spoke. At first glance, I am sure many of us would have been awestruck and reverent at the sight of him. Although he didn't wear any fancy clothing, *he was clothed with the glorious Power of the Most High.* Just by his demeanour, you could catch a glimpse of the hidden untold story of Elijah's walk with God; that Elijah loved the Lord and had been in conversations with Him many times before his first documented prophecy. And when you read his story, you will see that *the Word of the Lord* carried prominence and great weight throughout Elijah's ministry. He was God's chosen *Word Carrier* and *Mantle Wearer.*

> "Show me a man who claims to carry the Revival Mantle, and I'll show you a man who is burning with it. For the Revival Anointing is God's Fire blazing in the one appointed to bear it.

What is the Spirit of Elijah?

In my *Revival (Glory Carriers) Mentorship* book, *'Chosen to Carry the Glory—Carry the Fire of Jesus,'* I establish key definitions for 'Revival' that give insight into the Great Move of God. One of those phrases is "the *Spirit* of Elijah,"[10] taken from the description used by the sons of the prophets at Jericho when they saw Elisha (Elijah's successor) returning with *the Revival Mantle of Elijah* resting upon him (2 Kings 2:5–15). Before this, Elisha had asked Elijah for a double portion of Elijah's Spirit. What Elisha was asking for was more than just *Power from God.* He was asking for an inheritance of the *impact, mindset, attitude, character and posture of the Revival Anointing* (2 Kings 2:9). In this case, it would be *the handing over* of the Mantle (passing the baton) from a spiritual father (Elijah) to a *discipled* son (Elisha)—from a mentor to a mentee.

About 820 years later, the essence and attributes of Elijah's Anointing would be carried in a new vessel, named John. When the angel Gabriel came to deliver *God's Message* to Zacharias (John's

father), he used the words 'Spirit and Power.' The angel wasn't changing anything; he was simply saying the same thing, but with added emphasis (Luke 1:13–17). This points to two important elements here about the Power of God resting upon a vessel:
- The *Power of the Anointing*, and
- The *Ambassadorship and Mandate* of the chosen vessel.

The Lord worked mightily in this way also, when He took from *the Spirit* (or Mantle and its intrinsic attributes) resting upon Moses and placed it on the seventy elders of Israel. However, this was *an impartation (not a handing over)* of the Mantle (Numbers 11:17–29).

By its very nature, *the Spirit and Power describes the synergy of vessel and Anointing—a Divine partnership wonderfully woven together by the Spirit of God,* clearly seen in Elijah's life. Within this God-ordained partnership, the Holy Spirit always requires an earthen vessel through whom He can work. The same harmony rests upon anyone *mantled with the Power of God:* he walks in step with, and in full dependence on, the Holy Ghost (Psalms 133, Isaiah 61:1–3, Jeremiah 1:4–10).

The Anointing of Elijah—the Mantle Wearer and Word Carrier

The Mantle always responds to the Word. That's why I say, "The Mantle Wearer is also a Word Carrier." Elijah's life exemplifies this for us. When you read 1 Kings 17–18, you see him not only prophesying, but also *obeying the Word*:
- Elijah prophesied to Israel's King Ahab that there would be no rain except at his word (1 Kings 17:1).
- When he had finished prophesying this Word, *another Word (from the Lord)* came to him, instructing him to go to the brook

Cherith (east of the Jordan River), where the ravens would feed him (1 Kings 17:2–6).

- After a long while, the brook dried up because there was no rain. *The Word of the Lord* then came to Elijah to go to Zarephath, which is about 160 kilometres north-west of Cherith. Zarephath, a town by the sea (to the west) was in the Phoenician Region and was not part of Israel. God sent Elijah there because the Lord had already prepared a woman there to provide sustenance for Elijah.

A side note:
Understanding the geographical setting of this event shows to us that God showed Grace and favour to a non-Israelite (a Gentile). Though she was not part of the people of God, the all-inclusive aspect of God's Revival embraced her. I have no doubt that after Elijah's temporary abode with her she would have made *Yahweh her God*.

Now, this poor widow had nothing but a small bit of flour and a small portion of oil left (1 Kings 17:8–16). By every human measure, she was helpless, and in no position to care for Elijah. But Elijah knew what the natural eye could not see: *the Power of the Word was alive and burning in his spirit.* Guided by that living Word, he approached her—and in that moment, recognised the very woman the Lord had spoken to him about.

1 Kings 17:14–16
For thus saith the LORD God of Israel, The barrel of meal shall not waste, neither shall the cruse of oil fail, until the day that the LORD sendeth rain upon the earth. And she went and did according to the saying of Elijah: and she, and he, and her house, did eat many days. And the barrel of meal wasted

not, neither did the cruse of oil fail, according to the Word of the LORD, which He spake by Elijah.

- After a while, the widow's son fell ill and died. Then Elijah cried out earnestly to God, and the Lord heard his voice, and revived and restored the child (1 Kings 17:17–24). This, in itself, reflects the condition of the Church, which has become cold and dead. Yet the earnest prayers of the Burning Ones can bring Revival and restoration to the Church. When the woman saw that her son was restored to her, she said to Elijah, "Now I know that you are a *man of God* and that the *Word of the Lord in your mouth is Truth*" (1 Kings 17:24). Undoubtedly, *Elijah carried God's authentic response because his heart was aligned with God's Mandate.*
- Then, the appointed time came for the Lord to send rain again (three years had already passed by this time). The Word of the Lord came to Elijah in the form of an *Instruction* to repair the Lord's Altar on Mount Carmel (South of Zarephath—facing the Great Sea to the west). Elijah was told to go to King Ahab and summon him with all the prophets of Baal and all the people of the Kingdom of Israel. They were to meet Elijah at Mount Carmel, at the sight of the broken-down Altar of God (1 Kings 18:1–19). It wasn't merely a task to repair the Altar; it was a *Divine Assignment* entrusted to the *Mantle Wearer—a mandate* for the turning of hearts. This is what *Revival truly looks like.*

> **REVIVAL TRUTH:**
> " The job to repair the Altar (of the hearts) is Divine Assignment given to the Mantle Wearer.

When Elijah Repaired the Altar

The time for Israel's Revival had come. Elijah, as *God's Anointed Forerunner*, was given his Revival Mandate to repair the Altar at Mount Carmel. Now at the site of the abandoned Altar, and being aware that the *promised Fire* would come, Elijah began his speech by confronting and rebuking Israel for her waywardness. "How long will you be stuck between two opinions? If *Yahweh Adonai* is God, then follow Him. But if Baal is, then follow him (1 Kings 18:21)." To prove this statement, Elijah proposed that the prophets of Baal prepare their sacrifice and call on their god. Elijah would do the same and call on the name of His God. Elijah then declared before the people, "The God who answers by Fire, *He alone is God.*" That was the *sign that would prove the true and Living God*. (1 Kings 18:23–39) This great showdown with the prophets of Baal would leave them wishing they had never taken up Elijah's challenge in the first place.

> **REVIVAL TRUTH:**
> "
> The Fire is ready to fall and is looking for a prepared and pleasing Altar.

So, the prophets of Baal got to work, preparing their altar and sacrifice. Then they began to call upon their false god with frantic vigour and wild frenzy…but no fire fell. This went on for hours, right up to the afternoon, yet still there was no sign. Exhausted and defeated, they gave up. And then it was Elijah's turn. *The hour of Revival had come.* Elijah sensed *the Moving* of the Spirit. *The Word he carried was about to reach its fulfilment.* The boldness and courage of the Spirit's Power gripped him as he postured himself to receive God's Fire. Led by the Spirit, Elijah then repaired the Altar.

> **REVIVAL TRUTH:**
>
> " The Revival Fire causes hearts to turn to God.

Hallelujah! God's Altar was no longer in its abandoned state. The Lord God beheld from Heaven with immense delight, as the man of God repaired the Altar and then presented the acceptable sacrifice, which he thoroughly drenched with water. The Altar and the offering upon it was now prepared and pleasing before the Lord. Then Elijah prayed, "Let it be known this day that thou art God in Israel, and that I am Thy servant, and that I have done all these things at Thy Word." As soon as Elijah had said these words, *Yahweh's* Fire fell upon the Altar and consumed everything upon it, including the water. When the people saw this, their hearts turned toward God and they bowed themselves and worshipped *Yahweh— the true God.*

It's important to highlight here that no man-made fire was allowed near the prepared Altar. This is another distinct feature of the Move of God. The Great Revival Mandate cannot be manufactured by human effort. No strange fire is allowed. Only the authentic Fire of God can rightfully claim the acceptable offering (1 Kings 18:20–39). In God's Revival Plan for Israel, Elijah's ministry was a necessary confrontation to turn the hearts of the children back to their true heart of worship towards Him. Both the water and the Fire of God, which baptised the Altar, caused the hearts of the leaders and the people to turn to God.

Through the *obedience* of one man, *a place* was made ready for the Lord's Fire. In the same manner, when we obey the leading of the Holy Ghost, we are presenting to the Lord *a prepared place and a prepared Altar.*

The Altar of Our Hearts

Before God can send *the Promised Fire,* the Altar of our hearts first needs to be repaired, and the acceptable sacrifice, made ready for the Lord. This requires *a spirit of obedience*—the ethos and discipline of the Revivalist. You may be hungry for Revival, but the Revival Fire will never fall upon forsaken, broken-down, man-driven worship. Broken-down worship is when devotion and prayer are neglected, and the Word no longer stirs your heart. Man-driven worship is when we insist on our own songs, methods, and timing—yet it cannot receive the tangibleness of the Glory. When worship is done our way, we block the very Power and Presence we claim to seek.

Church, we are spiritually bankrupt without the Holy Ghost. I urge you to cultivate awareness of the Word of Glory, embracing *the discipline and attitude of obedience*. The Fire is ready to fall—it seeks a prepared, pleasing Altar. That Altar is one of *a contrite heart* and *obedience* (Isaiah 66:1–2, Psalms 51:16–17). It's an Altar ready to worship God at all times, and only on such an Altar will the Revival Fire descend.

Prayer:
Lord, we turn our hearts to You. Let Your Fire fall upon our hearts. Mighty God, consume us with the Glory of Your Word. In Jesus' Name, Amen…

May the Spirit And Power of Elijah Rest Upon You On the Day of the Great Awakening!

ENDNOTE:
10. (Sabadi, N.M.T, 2023. Preface, *Chosen to Carry the Glory—Carry the Fire of Jesus*, Norman Sabadi Publishing, Rockhampton, Queensland, Australia p.17).

*The Spirit and Power of Elijah
will be the shaking of
complacent, self-absorbed leaders
and the wandering, slumbering
sheep of the Church.*

CHAPTER 12

The Prophetic Continuation of the Revival Theme

Behold, I will send you Elijah the Prophet.

The 'Malachi 4:4-6 Prophecy' is a pivotal message for the Church, demanding our full attention and correct response, for it holds profound significance for God's plan for the Great Revival Mandate. The prophecy contains both a *promise of Revival* and a *prophetic continuation of the Spirit of the Revivalist*. All of these are part of the Lord's Divine strategy concerning the unfolding plan for Revival.

The Mount Carmel event serves as a *foreshadowing* and *typification* of the Great Revival Fire—a theme later entrusted to the Church. As God's Prophetic Testament, it *spoke again*, through John and Jesus, and eventually through the Church. When it finally reached the Church, the outpouring of the Holy Spirit brought increased spiritual insight and heightened awareness of the Glory of God amongst His people (Acts 2:17). This Revival Revelation was given so that the saints could enter into *a deeper, intimate understanding of the Ways of the Glory of God*.

And that is God's intent, that this precious Revelation should descend on us like soaking *Dew*. The Church was ordained for this *Clothing of Power*—to first be *washed by the Words of the Spirit* then and be *clothed with the Fire of God* (which is the correct order of Revival's Theme). Mount Carmel's pattern was also highlighted in John's message to the people (Note the bolded words),

Matthew 3:11
I indeed baptize you with water unto repentance: but He that cometh after me is mightier than I, whose shoes I am not worthy to bear: **He shall baptize you with the Holy Ghost, and with Fire:**

The Revival Theme

Malachi 4:4–6
Remember ye the law of Moses My servant, which I commanded unto him in Horeb for all Israel, with the statutes and judgments. Behold, I will send you Elijah the prophet before the coming of the great and dreadful Day of the LORD: And he shall turn the heart of the fathers to the children, and the heart of the children to their fathers, lest I come and smite the earth with a curse.

From what we have learnt from the previous chapter on the *spirit and Power of Elijah*, where Malachi said, "I send you Elijah the prophet," is THE REVIVAL THEME. God was going to send the same *Revival Power* and its attributes through chosen vessels, prepared just like Elijah was prepared.

Also, the prophet Malachi was stating more than meets the eye. The prophecy referenced the Mount Carmel event, whether Malachi was aware of this or not—the *Revival Theme and Pattern was established there* (1 Kings 18). Let me outline this for you to see:

- The Revivalist receives the Word and obeys it,
- The Revivalist gathers the people and gives them prophetic exhortation,
- The (Revivalist) Forerunner testifies of the coming Fire,
- Altars of true worship to *Yahweh* are repaired,
- A prepared sacrifice (the offering of our hearts),
- The Altar is drenched in water—representing the washing of the Word (sanctified as a pleasing offering),
- The Altar is consumed by the Fire of God—representing the Glory/Revival Fire in our midst,
- The Forerunner witnesses the Fire, and
- The people witness the Fire—hearts turn to God.

> **REVIVAL TRUTH:**
>
> "The spirit and Anointing of Elijah always prepares the way for the Fire of God to come.

The pattern of the Revival Theme and the essence and purpose of the Revivalist Mantle would later continue in John's life as *Christ's forerunner and the hosting Revivalist*. Like Elijah, John was to prepare the hearts of people (the Altar) for the coming Christ (the sacrifice and the One who baptises with the Fire of God).

Do you see it already? *The Revivalist Anointing is a Forerunner Anointing.* So the Great Revival Fire is going to be received and hosted by a chosen Fire Carrier. Friends, the spirit and Anointing of

Elijah (The Revivalist) always prepare the way for the Fire of God to come. That's why it is of great importance that you recognise the Fire Carriers in your midst. They will mentor and lead you to the Blessing of the Great Revival Fire.

The Rise of the Burning Ones

When the Fire of God rests upon the Church, this will be more than just *an improvement*. It will be *Revival transformation and reformation*, where the repairing of hearts happens and the Glory is *welcomed* in the midst of God's people.

Now, contentions might rise in the Church about who really is a Revivalist. But for your sakes, let me state again the key component of the criteria that marks a true Revivalist. **A Baptism of Fire must first mark you before you can lead God's people.** *The Spirit and Power of Elijah is the identifying Mark.* God is no respecter of persons on the matter. Whom He chooses, He has chosen. That is why I stated earlier: the clergy of the Church are not *Revival leaders* unless a Revival Anointing rests upon them.

In view of this thought, *if we are to welcome the Glory, we must first welcome the Glory Carriers in our midst.* That's the way the Lord has chosen to work.

The current clergy must therefore recognise and accept *the Leaders of the Move.* Whether they like this or not, the shaking of the Church will come through, and only through God's appointed *Burning Ones.* These anointed individuals carry the same heart posture and Revival ethos as their Revival forefathers—Elijah and John. The prophetic utterance of the Spirit is strong upon them. God has anointed them with a Revival Anointing to be forerunners of His Promised Outpouring. The sooner this adjustment happens, the sooner the Lord will work to shake the Church and the nations.

> **REVIVAL TRUTH:**
>
> " If we are to welcome the Glory, we must first welcome the Glory Carrier in our midst.

Consider that Mount Carmel wouldn't have happened without Elijah's submission to the Word. Likewise, the Jordan River (with John), and the Upper Room (with the hundred and twenty disciples of Jesus).

Indeed, the Glory of the Lord will burn upon *Anointed Ones* to set the pace for God-encounters. These appointed *Revivalists* will teach the Church her true worship posture, and her prophetic characteristics (John 4:23–24). They will be used by the Lord to prepare the hearts of the people to receive the coming Great Fire of God. *Revivalist fathers* will be led by the Spirit to raise *Revivalist sons*. The spiritual sons (the Joshuas, Calebs and Elishas) will also be summoned to respond to their *Burning Bush—Upper Room encounter*.

The Great Stirring—A Prophetic Confrontation

"The Move of God shall be ignited through the Spirit of Prophecy.

A great prophetic stirring is coming and is going to cause a powerful awakening in the Church. This *prophetic confrontation* from the Holy Spirit is going to dislodge and dismantle fleshly works in the Church. The Spirit will call for a yielding amongst the leaders, and this yielding will *overflow* to the sheep. A yielding to what exactly?... The prophetic identity and prophetic functions of the Church. Because you can't have Revival without prophetic utterance and prophetic manifestations (ignited and stirred by the Holy Spirit).

And because the Spirit is postured for Revival, He will address the heart posture of the current leaders of the Church to break from them a religious spirit and give them sight to see and ears to hear (1 Corinthians 2:9–12). By *Prophetic Confrontation*, I mean the people of God will be stirred to prophesy. The spiritual Elijahs (The Revival leaders) will, by the Moving of the Spirit, confront the Ahabs (clergy—fathers of our day (Isaiah 49:22–23, 1 Kings 17:1). The Anointing of the Revivalist is a strong prophetic Mantle, and is postured to disrupt and interfere with the Church's current practices.

The Spirit of Prophecy will be relentless, forthright and powerful. He must, if the Church is going to receive His Glory. Leaders are going to be prophesied at, and many in the Body of Christ, including leaders themselves, are going to be stirred by the Spirit to give *prophetic utterances*.

Now, what does it mean to be *prophetic?* By its true definition, anyone who is prophetic hears from God, sees by the enabling of the Spirit and proclaims what the Spirit stirs them to say. *Prophetic means coming from God, and is of God*—with God as the source of the Word received.

> **REVIVAL TRUTH:**
> " A holy confrontation from the Holy Spirit is going to dislodge and dismantle fleshly works in the Church.

Putting it all together, the Move of God is about the Glory of the Word received and proclaimed through earthen vessels. That is why I said earlier, "You can't have Revival without prophetic utterance and prophetic manifestations."

Prophecy in the old times didn't come by the will of man, but holy vessels of God spoke as they were *moved by the Holy Ghost*. Now that same blessing has come to us. Many will be moved by the Holy Ghost to speak and they won't cease until the *Burden of the Word* is fulfilled (2 Peter 1:21). This is also characteristic of the Revivalist Mantle, which is *fully prophetic*. In fact, everything about the Anointing (any Anointing) is prophetic.

This kind of stirring releases *authentic prophecy*. By authentic, I mean whatever they speak will come to pass. If they prophesy evil, it will come to pass. If they prophesy good, it will come to pass. They speak because they are moved by the Holy Ghost (2 Peter 1:20–21).

In a program-based Church, prophetic utterance stirred up by the Holy Ghost is going to disrupt meetings and cause leaders to react to it; either with receptiveness or they will despise it and attempt to shut it down. This is where the prophetic confrontation will happen—a confrontation between man-led worship and Spirit-led, Spirit-inspired worship. The good news is, the fervour and zeal of the Spirit will persist until a full handing over of control to the Holy Spirit happens. This is going to take place because of the heightened prophetic activity in the Church.

God is calling leaders to become hosting ministers of the Glory of the Lord—*to host the prophetic Word and the Glory of the Word*. For the Glory of *the Latter Rain* will come. It will be combined with the Glory of *the Former Rain*, and the Blessing upon the Church will be phenomenal (Joel 2:23, Zechariah 10:1). When this era of the Great Outpouring is upon the Church, *the Sound Revival, which is the Prophetic Voice of the Spirit,* will be heard across the land. For the Lord's Glory will speak—with Power and Peace. He will speak until He fills His people with the Glory of His Word.

Now is the time... The Spirit of Prophecy—the Spirit of the Move is already stirring a prophetic people to respond correctly. They will turn with all their hearts because of the Glory of the Word, flowing through *God's chosen Burning Ones and Revival Leaders.*

Prayer:
Dear Jesus, you are the King of Glory. Please forgive us for not receiving your chosen vessels, who have carried the Glory of Your Word to us. We now turn our hearts to you, and we humble ourselves before you. Lord, we bow down and worship you with contriteness in our hearts. For Jesus, you are the King of Glory. Come Holy Spirit and have your way in us.

Amen...

May Your Heart Be Glad to Receive the Day of the Great Awakening!

The Prophetic Continuation of The Revival Theme CHAPTER 12

I bare record that a Great Fire of Revival is about to descend upon the people of God.

CHAPTER 13

The Spirit & Power of Elijah in John the Baptist

"I baptise you with water, but there is One who is coming after me. He will baptise you with the Holy Ghost and Fire."
— **John the Baptist (Luke 3:16)**

John the Baptist came in the Spirit and Power of Elijah. John shared the *resemblance* of the Revival Theme. Like Elijah, he was God's *appointed forerunner* who would prepare the hearts of the people to receive Yeshua the Messiah (*the Altar of God, the ultimate sacrifice,* and the *Baptiser of the Fire of God*).

John 1:32–34

And John bare record, saying, I saw the Spirit descending from heaven like a dove, and it abode upon Him. And I knew Him not: but He that sent me to baptise with water, the same said unto me, upon Whom thou shalt see the Spirit descending, and remaining on Him, the same is He which baptiseth with the Holy Ghost. And I saw, and bare record that this is the Son of God.

The angel Gabriel, when speaking to Zacharias (John's father), referenced Malachi's prophecy and proclaimed that the Revival Theme would continue in John's life. John *would come beforehand as Christ's forerunner*. Gabriel resonated with the Prophet Malachi's prophecy about *the sending of Elijah*. He (John) was to go before Him (Jesus Christ) in the spirit and Power of Elijah, to turn the hearts of the fathers to the children, and the disobedient to the wisdom of the just, to make ready a people prepared for the Lord (Zechariah 1:2–3, Luke 1:11–17, Malachi 4:5–6). Zacharias (John's father) also prophesied the *forerunner* aspect of John's ministry:

Luke 1:76–79

And thou, child, shalt be called the prophet of the Highest: for thou shalt go before the Face of the Lord to prepare His ways; To give knowledge of salvation unto His people by the remission of their sins, through the tender mercy of our God; whereby the Dayspring from on High hath *visited us*, to give Light to them that sit in darkness and in the shadow of death, to guide our feet into *the way of Peace*.

John, as *Christ's forerunner*, fulfilled the prophecies made by his father and that of the prophet Isaiah (Isaiah 40:3–5, Matthew 3:1–3) John, like Elijah, was preparing the hearts of the people to receive a baptism of encounter and Fire.

Matthew 3:11

I indeed baptize you with water unto repentance: but He that cometh after me is mightier than I, whose Shoes I am not worthy to bear: He shall baptize you with the Holy Ghost, and with Fire:

An interesting fact:

The meaning of the name *Jordan* means "*to flow down or descending.*" And that is exactly what happened at Mount Carmel, with the flowing water and the descending Fire. The *pattern* of the Revival Theme of Mount Carmel was clearly visible in the flowing waters of Jordan and the Baptism of the Spirit descending upon Jesus, the Messiah.

The Similarities Between Elijah & John

John continued the ethos, mandate and disciplines of *the Revivalist Mantle*. He was a *Mantle Wearer* and *Word Carrier* just like Elijah. The Revival Theme, landmarked at Mount Carmel through Elijah resounded again at the Jordan River through John. This was the continuing motif of *God's unfolding plan for Revival*. The essence of the Revival Message was comprised of two significant elements —to be *baptised in the Water of God* and to be *baptised in the Fire of God* (John 3:5).

You can see the resemblance of Mount Carmel's pattern identifiable in John, who also had to obey God's directives about repairing a different type of altar—that Altar was the hearts of the people. Just like Elijah was led by the Spirit to drench the Altar with water, John was appointed by God to immerse people into the waters of the Jordan (Matthew 3:13–17). Whether John was aware of this or not, he was preparing the *New Altar* for the Fire of God to descend upon it, and to *baptise or anoint it. (Jesus being the foundation and exemplar of the new way).*

After John had *immersed* Jesus in the water, as Jesus came up out of the water, the Holy Spirit then descended upon Him. This same Holy Spirit was *the Baptismal Fire* that John spoke of. It was a different kind of Fire from that of Mount Carmel's—this was *the Fire that Anoints man* (Mark 1:8, Luke 3:16). Immediately in that moment, *the Mantle of the Anointed One came upon Jesus.* The imagery of this open vision which John received was amazing. John saw the Spirit descend *like a dove* (not a dove, but like a dove). Visually, it would have looked like *a white Mantle (Coat)* spread out like wings, which when it fell, then rested on the man, Jesus. **The baptismal Fire anoints—the Spirit of Christ anoints.** There in the waters of *Jordan* (meaning to flow down or descend), John *witnessed* the Power of the Spirit descending and resting upon *the Anointed Saviour* and he heard the Words of the Father saying, "This is My Son in Whom I am well pleased." What a powerful prophetic event this was. The appointed Revival had come to the people and was standing before them in the Jordan River, *embodied and received in the person*—Jesus Christ, with John as *His forerunner-witness.* Furthermore, it wasn't just empowerment from the Spirit, God was *well pleased* with the offering of Jesus—the New Altar…

In the next chapter, I will introduce to you what I call, *"The hidden Gem of Revival."*

Prayer:
Blessed Saviour, bring to us the miracle of Your Words and cause the Power of Your Spirit to Move upon us. Lord, we are ready to receive Your Blessed Fire.
In Jesus Name,
Amen…

May the Revival Fire Carried From Elijah to John Be Upon You, As You Receive the Glory of the Great Awakening!

PART 6   *The Elijah Mantle: Preparing the Way Again*

TABLE: THE REVIVAL THEME FROM ELIJAH TO JOHN

Mount Carmel	Jordan River
Elijah the Prophet	John the Prophet
Mantle Wearer and Word Carrier	Mantle Wearer and Word Carrier
Elijah obeys the Word to repair the Altar and turn the hearts of the people back to God	John obeys the Word to repair the hearts of the people by turning them back to God
Forerunner to the Fire of God that Baptised the Altar	Forerunner to the Christ, who baptises with Fire
Elijah prepared the Altar of God and Drenched it in water	John prepared the hearts of the people and baptised in water. John Baptised Jesus in Water.
Elijah called the meeting at Mount Carmel and repaired the Altar by God's Directive. He was OBEYING God's instructions to fulfil the purpose of righteousness.	When Jesus came to Jordan to be baptised by John, He told John to go ahead with baptising Him, because they were OBEYING God's Instructions to fulfil the purpose of righteousness.
Elijah witnessed the Fire of God descend upon the prepared Altar and Baptise the Altar. God was pleased with the Altar and the Sacrifice upon the Altar.	John saw the Spirit of God (Fire of God) descend on Jesus like a dove) and John heard the Voice of the Father saying, "This is my son in whom I am well pleased." God was pleased with the Altar and the Sacrifice upon the Altar.
Then Elijah prophesied rain was coming, and rain did come at God's Appointed Time.	John did prophesy also that the Christ would come and He would have the 'Spirit without measure.' (John 3:34) Christ then Poured the Spirit without measure upon the Church and God's Commanded Blessing came upon the Upper Room as the appointed DEW of Heaven (Psalms 133, Acts 2:1)

The Spirit & Power of Elijah In John The Baptist   CHAPTER 13

Your part in His Story is very important.

CHAPTER 14

'Yohannan'

Grace and Truth found me.

Now picture this scene—Heaven holding its breath with immense joy and delight, as Jesus stood before John in the Jordan River. Religious minds failed to see it. But there it was... Grace and Truth stepped out of eternity and fixed His eyes upon imperfect humanity. The Word became of low estate and met man at his gaze and said to him, "Yohannan—you're the one—We chose you!"

Let me explain in more detail. John bore witness and testified of the marvellous revelation of Christ because he also was impacted greatly by *Grace and Truth*.

> **John 1:15–17 (John's the Baptist's words)**
> ...This was He of whom I spake, He that cometh after me is preferred before me: for He was before me. And of *His fulness* have all we received, and *Grace for Grace*. For the law was given by Moses, but *Grace and Truth came by Jesus Christ*.

PART 6   *The Elijah Mantle: Preparing the Way Again*

At the Jordan River as Jesus stood before John, His *forerunner*, it was clear from John's words to Jesus that John didn't think highly of himself—he considered himself *a nobody before God*. He preferred Jesus above himself. Earlier, when John was preaching to a crowd of people he told them that while even the lowest of servants can undo their master's shoelace, such a place was one of *honour* that was still too high for him. He stated that he wasn't worthy to undo the Messiah's shoelaces. John considered it appropriate to seek after the lesser role. His maxim was clear and defined, "I must decrease, but He must increase… *He must* (John 3:30)."

> **REVIVAL TRUTH:**
> "The true work of Revival is with Grace and Truth, Peace and Power.

Yet, when Christ stood before John in the waters of the Jordan, His gaze communicated a deeper Truth to John, "I can't fulfil this by myself John. *Your part in this is established by the Father and is very important.*"

(My reflections to the Forerunner) "Oh, John, I want you to see the work of Grace and Truth on display. God is not only well-pleased with His Son…but hear me—*He is pleased with you too.*"

I have pondered on what my first words might be to John when I get to finally meet him (in Heaven). This is what I think I would say to him, "Blessed are you *Yohannan*, oh Elijah of God! You saw the One who baptises with Fire and you knew it was Him, because you carried a true posture of brokenness and authentic worship before *Yeshua*, the Anointed One. John…the meaning of Elijah's (*Eliyahu's*) name is—my God is *Yahweh!* And God did proclaim its meaning at Mount Carmel. And yours is *Yohannan*—my God is *Gracious!* It is of equal significance that God proclaimed the meaning of your name at the Jordan River. You were named *Yohannan* for a reason because God was going to demonstrate *the Revival Message of His Grace and Truth* in the Jordan River. That message was not only for those in your generation, but for every generation that followed after you. That's why Jesus called you, 'The greatest prophet.' You might be wondering what that message was, that you delivered for our sakes? It was this:

> Abundant Grace met with me face to face, Mercy has accepted my heart's posture, and Glory chose to reveal Himself to me. I was given the Blessing to partake of His holy Mandate. The Lord has shone His Countenance upon me, even if I thought less of myself. I was chosen to receive, host, and release His Revival Testimony. I was chosen to be a part of His Glory Mandate.

And all of this became true only because *Grace and Truth stood before you and embraced you*—that is you... Yohannan—*My God is Gracious!"* That is your testimony.

Now, the crescendo of this powerful message must resonate in our hearts as the new generation of Glory Carriers. May we also see ourselves in that same light—*Grace and Truth found us.* Let "My God is gracious" be our testimony too.

A moment of reflection:
Grace and Truth is standing before you to embrace you. God has found you worthy to be marked with His Fire... Grace and Truth have found you.

When you really step into the situation, what Jesus was saying to John, was "Grace has called you to do this. Yohannan, you were chosen to stand before Me and to be a *witness to this Holy Moment* (Luke 1:76–79)." I am awestruck because the Father in Heaven was not only honouring Jesus, He was also honouring *John's part in the whole story.* The Aaronic Blessing was being demonstrated in this event and John was the recipient of this Blessing.

Numbers 6:24–27

...The LORD bless thee, and keep thee: The LORD make His Face shine upon thee, and BE GRACIOUS UNTO THEE: The LORD lift up His Countenance upon thee, and give thee Peace. And they shall put My Name upon the children of Israel; and I will Bless them.

Friends, what happened to John is also for all of us. The work of Grace and Truth can meet you wherever you are right now. Consider how the prophet Isaiah, as he beheld the Glory of God, was gripped with great conviction, similar to that of John's, and he said, "Woe is me for I am undone, for I am a man of unclean lips" (Isaiah 6:1–7). The fact that he was granted the opportunity to behold the Glory was the work of Grace and Truth embracing Him.

John had the same posture before the Lord (Isaiah 66:1–2). He said, "My Lord, I need to be baptised by You." I picture in my mind how that scene would've played out, how John surely would have bowed himself low before Christ the King and almost have dipped himself into the water. Yet, Christ reached forward and raised him up, as if to say, "Yohannan, this is your part, and the Father and I can't do it without you."

> **REVIVAL TRUTH:**
>
> " God looks at the heart of man when He picks His Revivalist. He also looks at that same heart when He uses him to demonstrate His Glory.

Hallelujah! I am left speechless with joyful tears. You can see *Grace and Truth* at work throughout the Bible, Enoch was taken by God because he pleased God; when Noah and his family were kept safe because Noah walked with God and obeyed His unusual commands. God's prophetic promise was spoken at Mount Moriah over Abraham and Isaac, to Bethel (as Jacob discovered that God was in that place, and God spoke with him there); and from the Burning Bush (where Moses met God) to the cleft of the Rock (where he found favour in God's sight and he saw the hind parts of the Glory). How marvellous it is that God's abundant Grace, wrapped up in Heavenly Truth, continues to be poured upon earthen vessels. It came upon the house of Jesse, when God picked a ruddy David because the Lord was pleased with him. *For David was a man after God's heart* (1 Samuel 13:14, 1 Samuel 16:7).

And then it was Yohannan's turn. He was standing before Christ —the Grace and Truth of God. God was embracing and affirming Yohannan's part in the Move of God.

In that same unifying message, the Spirit wants you to be a part of the Glory Move. Grace and Truth are before you now, and the Spirit is calling you to a holy place in Him. As unwanted and unloved as you may feel, you are highly valued in God's eyes. As broken and as useless as you may think you are, *God wants to mark you with His Revival Anointing.* God calls you His chosen. You might not count yourself worthy, but He does. You may feel unloved, defeated, disqualified and downtrodden. You may feel lost (in the Church), struggling to find a place amongst God's people. On top of that, you might have sensed the gaze of judging eyes, who have already written you off and labelled you as an outcast. You might even have said to yourself, "I am okay with accepting this crippling condition," so as not to cause offence with the clergy and draw unnecessary attention to yourself. Sadly, you are left serving the role of warming the pews. Yet, the Spirit of Christ is before you and He says, "There is more for you, My son and daughter…there is more!" You are not meant to be outside of *the Plan of God*. You are a part of the Great Revival Story—*the Story of Grace and Truth*. Bow low before Him. Lay your brokenness and inadequacy at His Feet. Then let His gaze rest on you.

A moment of reflection:
Jesus's Baptism at the Jordan River was *a full message with a full story*—John was included in that story. And this coming Great Revival Mandate is a full message with a full story—you are included in His Story. This is not just His Story, it is yours too. And you're going to *make History with Him*.

I speak to you, *forerunners of God*, your time of hiding in the wilderness is almost up, and the time of your revealing has come. Know that you're not going to do this alone because the Power of Christ is with you—in you and upon you. Christ has come to restore the hearts of the people to God. But He wants you to be a part of His Story, just like *Yohannan*. Friends… Grace and Truth will find you and mark you with a powerful Revival Anointing. Grace and Truth will give you a place in the Army of God to fulfil your part in the Great Revival Mandate.

Yohannan—My God is Gracious!

May We Declare With One Voice, On His Glory-Day, "Grace and Truth Have Found Us!"

'Yohannan'   CHAPTER 14

"For John truly baptised with water; but ye shall be baptised with the Holy Ghost not many days hence." — *Acts 1:5*

CHAPTER 15

The Spirit & Power of Elijah in the Church

His Glory shall be seen in you.

At the Mount of Olives, the hour had come for Jesus to ascend into Heaven. But before He departed, the Lord gave His disciples a final charge: Go to Jerusalem, and wait—wait for the *Promised Fire* of the Holy Spirit (Acts 1:4–8). *The Dawn of the New Day* of the Church was approaching. It was time for the disciples to be mantled with Power for the Revival Mandate.

A humble hiding place called the Upper Room in Jerusalem became the meeting point between God and man. That quiet *place* was marked by Heaven, and would erupt as the birthplace *of* the Spirit's Outpouring—t*he first Great Awakening of the Church would ignite there.* In God's Revival plan, this was the beginning—the first of many *Fire-Baptisms to come* (Acts 2). Just as on Mount Carmel, just as at the Jordan River, the Upper Room was chosen for a *Divine Visitation, a Divine Marking. It would blaze like the Burning Bush—at Heaven's appointed time.*

Back at the Mount of Olives, the disciples might have thought differently as they heard Jesus deliver His final instructions before ascending into Heaven. Their hearts were troubled—they were more concerned with the fact that Jesus was leaving them, and they wanted to know when He would return. They wanted signs; they wanted certainty. But they did not yet understand that Jesus was establishing His *Ecclesia (Church—an Assembly or gathering of believers called out from the world, to be established with Power in Him)*. While the disciples were focused on *Jesus's Second Coming,* Jesus was focused on *The Holy Spirit's Coming—the Revival Outpouring* that would soon sweep the Earth after His Departure. He had spoken of this before, in many conversations (John 7:38-39, John 14:12–18, John 16:4–15). And now the Time had come! Jesus declared prophetically, "…ye shall be Baptised with the Holy Ghost not many days hence (Acts 1:3–5)."

A moment of reflection:
This is exactly what the Spirit is also saying to us concerning the coming Great Revival Fire. "Not many days from now, it will be your turn to receive His Promised Endowment."

After Jesus had ascended, the disciples made their way back to Jerusalem to wait for *the Coming of the Holy Spirit.* I imagined their quiet conversations along the way—their hearts heavy with the reality that Jesus was no longer with them in person. And yet deep within, they knew they had to be ready—to receive the Promise. They clung to His Words, knowing the Spirit was coming. As they drew closer to Jerusalem, I could feel their anticipation… What would *this Special Endowment* look like? How would Heaven's Power come upon them?

A hundred and twenty had gathered in that Upper Room—because they remembered His Words, "Not many days hence…

(Acts 1:5)." They also held fast to His promise, "I will not leave you *comfortless:* I will come to you" (John 14:18)..."*I will send you the Comforter*" (John 16:7)! This was it—this was the very event Jesus was speaking of. The moment Heaven had been waiting for was now at hand!

John 14:15–18

If ye love Me, keep My commandments. And I will pray the Father, and He shall give you another Comforter, that **He may abide with you for ever; Even the Spirit of truth;** whom the world cannot receive, because it seeth Him not, neither knoweth Him: but ye know Him; **for He dwelleth with you, and shall be in you. I will not leave you comfortless: I will come to you.**

A wonderful point to note:

It is striking that Jesus said He Himself would come to us—and we see that He would do this through His Holy Spirit. Jesus, through the Spirit, was not coming merely to visit and then depart. No… He was coming to abide with us forever.

Persecution was standing at the door—yet the disciples *remained obedient!* They followed through with Christ's instructions to wait in Jerusalem, even before they fully understood what it would mean. Then, Jesus's Words became a living reality within them. They rose as *Living Witnesses,* endowed with Christ's Power, ready to carry the Fire of God into the world! That quiet Upper Room—shifted from ordinary to supernatural—when Heaven invaded, it became *God's Holy Altar,* blazing with *the Fire of the Holy Ghost.* And when the Fire blazed within them, it pierced through the thickness of religion, shattered the chains of sin, and shook hearts to their very core—drawing multitudes to Jesus. From that holy Birthplace of Power, the Fire Carriers went forth, clothed with the Glory of Christ, and with His Words burning in their hearts—with unshakeable intent.

Reflecting on the Revival Theme at Mount Carmel, when Elijah *witnessed* the Fire fall on the Altar, the Theme echoed once more at the Jordan River, when John *saw* the Spirit—the Baptismal Fire—descend upon Jesus. But for the saints, theirs was an upgrade! They were not spectators of the spectacular; they were called to become *Living Witnesses* of the endowing Fire that would *descend upon them*—just like Jesus. As soon as they were *clothed, they rose as Word Carriers* and *Mantle Wearers*, following in the footsteps of their Revival Fathers. The Glory that filled the Upper Room was not only around them—it rested upon them like dew from Heaven, becoming within them *the Fire of God's Word, postured to shake the nations.*

> "The saints were baptised with the Fire…and they testified with the Fire resting on them—That is Revival.

A side note:

Elijah and John indeed were mantled with a powerful Revival Mantle. Yet, their roles at Mount Carmel (Elijah) and the Jordan River (John) were not the final destination—they were prophetic signposts, pointing to a greater reality. That greater reality is THE CHURCH. Both witnessed the Fire descend upon the Altar—Elijah with a literal Flame from Heaven, and John with the endowing Power of the Spirit upon Christ. But when their parts are combined with Jesus's part—He, the true Altar that receives the Fire—we see the full message of REVIVAL. That message is twofold: to

Witness the Fire, and to become Glory Carriers—vessels endowed with that very same Fire.

As I have stated earlier, Jesus's Baptism at the Jordan River, modelled the full pattern of Revival, revealing two essential elements:

- To be baptised with *Water (Discipled in the Word),* and
- To be baptised with *Fire (Endowed with the Spirit).*

When Jesus received the Fire—His Mantle as Christ—He stepped forward to continue His Ministry as a Carrier of the Fire (Acts 10:38). And He desired that His disciples would fully grasp *this truth:* that they were called to take on the Glorying-carrying nature He established. The Church, as God's redeemed Glory-Carrier, would now become the *New Altar, and their willing hearts—the Acceptable Sacrifice* before God (Isaiah 60:7; Malachi 1:11).

> "Only a prepared Altar—an Altar of humility and love for God can receive the Fire of the Holy Ghost.

Man—the New Altar

Through Jesus, man became the Altar that carries the Fire. This was God's design from the beginning in Genesis, and this is what He desired for the Church. Jesus became for us 'the Cleft of the Rock'—*a place of acceptance and encounter*—so that we may now come boldly and behold the Glory of God, our Father (Hebrews 4:14–16). Hallelujah!

The unmatched wisdom of God is so profound in its depth—astounding and beyond comprehension. Long before the Upper Room, God was already speaking through the prophets about the *New Altar and the pouring out of His Spirit.* For hundreds of years, the intent of what was to come was already in God's Heart, waiting for His appointed time.

- **Moses:** Beginning with the prophet Moses, who spoke of this some 1400 years before Christ, he told his spiritual son, Joshua, "...Enviest thou for my sake? Would God that *all the Lord's people* were prophets, and that **the Lord would put His Spirit upon them!** (Numbers 11:29)." Even then, God was revealing His plan for His Spirit to rest on the people.
- **Isaiah:** About 770 years before the Upper Room, God revealed to the prophet Isaiah, "...they shall come with acceptance on My Altar, and I will glorify the House of My Glory." Even then, God was pointing to the *Day* when His people would become *Living Altars.*
- **Joel:** About 500 years before the Upper Room, God then revealed through the prophet Joel, proclaiming, "**I shall pour out My Spirit upon all flesh**, and your sons and daughters shall prophesy (Joel 2:13, 28–29, Isaiah 60:7)." Even then, God was showing that His Outpouring would not be limited to a few.
- **Haggai:** About 400 years before the Upper Room, God spoke through the prophet Haggai "...I will shake all nations, and the desire of all nations shall come: and **I will fill this House with Glory**... The Glory of this latter House shall be greater than of the former...and in **this Place will I give Peace,** saith the LORD of hosts (Haggai 2:6–9)."
- **Malachi:** Also about 400 years before the Upper Room, the Lord spoke through the prophet Malachi, saying, "For from the rising of the sun even unto the going down of the same My Name shall be great among the Gentiles; **and in every place incense shall be offered unto My name, and a pure offering:** for My Name shall be great among the heathen, saith the LORD of hosts (Malachi 1:11).

All these prophets spoke as they were moved by the Holy Spirit (2 Peter 1:20–21). This was not a random idea. The All-Knowing God was at work to accomplish *His desire in mankind*. He intended for the Power of the Spirit to rest upon earthen vessels, so that His *Glory would be seen in them* (Isaiah 60:1–3).

> "The Glory in our midst, is the Promised Land of our holy inheritance—We are chosen to be clothed with His Glory.

Therefore, the Holy Spirit's work in us, is not just mere religion. Rather, *He must Move us with His Words* (John 7:38–39). The best part is that, no longer is the Fire to rest only on a few, like Elijah and John. But through Jesus Christ, the Holy Spirit is now made available to *all flesh* (note the bolded).

Acts 2:16–18

But this is that which was spoken by the prophet Joel; And it shall come to pass in the last days, saith God, **I will pour out of My Spirit upon all flesh: and your sons and your daughters shall prophesy**, and your young men shall see visions, and your old men shall dream dreams: And on My servants and on My handmaidens I will pour out in those days of My Spirit; and they shall prophesy:

Now that you know this Truth, it's time for you to align with His Word to *host His Glory*. Let the Altar of our hearts be fully given to the Holy Spirit. For the Lord wants to *Anoint you with His Glory*. Arise! *Ye Gates and let the King of Glory come in.*

Psalms 24:7

Lift up your heads, O ye gates; and be ye lift up, ye everlasting doors; and the King of Glory shall come in.

"...I will come to you (John 14:18)...and I will perform My good Word toward you...(Jeremiah 29:10)."

A relevant point to note:

The prophets prophesied about the Revival Mandate right up to Jesus. The apostles, who walked with Jesus, received insight of it by the Spirit, and they taught on it. The apostle Paul said, "We are built upon *the foundation* of the apostles and prophets, Jesus Christ Himself being the Chief Corner Stone; In whom all the Building (which is us), fitly framed together, grows unto **an Holy Temple in the Lord: In whom you also are built together for an Habitation of God through the Spirit** (Ephesians 2:20–22)"... Paul was not talking about the office/calling of the apostles and the prophets. Rather, it was *what they proclaimed*. He was talking about God's Revival Plan—*The foundation and its framework is the Revival Mandate of God* (it's right there in the statement...in bold).

Reconciliation—Redemption—Glory

God didn't just reconcile us and redeem us, **He wanted His Glory to abide with us and in us.** The apostle Paul received deep revelation on this. He, being led by the Spirit, said (Romans 8:28–30):

- God *knew us* before time ever began (Jeremiah 1:4–5),

- God *ordained and predestined* our redemption through Christ Jesus (He authored our faith and He shall also complete our faith journey—Hebrew 12:2),
- God *called us*, (and gave us a special invitation to be one with Him. He stirred us to *First Love*) (Isaiah 41:4, John 12:32, John 17),
- God *justified us* through Christ Jesus (Acts 13:39, Romans 3:21–26, 1 Corinthians 6:11),
- He *will indeed, Glorify us* (by the Power of His Spirit resting upon us) (Isaiah 60:7, Haggai 2:6–9).

The Glory Shall Be Visible In Us

"We shall be like Him, for we shall see Him as He is"

—Apostle John (1 John 3:2)

The Glory intended that He would be visible in the Church—visible through the endowing Power of the Anointing resting upon us. And the Fire of God must continually burn in us until the fullness of Christ is radiating in full strength through us. That's what "Glory to Glory" means (2 Corinthians 3:17-18). Additionally, it isn't a glory that acts independently of God. Rather, it is the Spirit emanating from us, revealing Christ through our beings, as God's *Latter House*.

The point I make here is that our continuous beholding of the Word of Glory (or Revival Fire) is changing us from Glory to Glory. The more we behold or fellowship with His Glory, the more we are being changed. The more we abide in the flowing Anointing of His Spirit, the more He becomes visible in us. (Note the bolded)

1 John 3:1–2

Behold, what manner of love the Father hath bestowed upon us, that we should be called the sons of God: therefore the world knoweth us not, because it knew Him not. Beloved, now are we the sons of God, and it doth not yet appear what we shall be: **but we know that, when He shall appear, we shall be like Him; for we shall see Him as He is.**

Romans 8:17–18

And if children, then heirs; heirs of God, and joint-heirs with Christ; if so be that we suffer with Him, that we may be also glorified together. **For I reckon that the sufferings of this present time are not worthy to be compared with the Glory which shall be revealed in us.**

So, we must persist, keeping our lamps filled with the Oil of His Holy Spirit. We must *burn unceasingly with His Revival Anointing,* like the Lampstand—the Menorah—in the Holy Place (Leviticus 24:1-4) until we reach the Final Day. And what a glorious conclusion it will be, when the Last Trumpet sounds and we shall at last be like our Lord Jesus, for we shall see Him as He is (1 John 3:2).

Prayer:

Lord we humble our hearts before you. Come Holy Spirit and let your Fire rest upon us. Burn so bright in us that Your Glory may be visible to all those around us. In Jesus Name, Amen…

May Jesus, the King of Glory, Fill His You With His Glory!

Part 7 – Fathering the Move of God

"Because you are lukewarm, I will spew you out of My Mouth... Repent."

CHAPTER 16

Lukewarmness, Fatherlessness Crisis, & the Turning of Hearts

When Revival Fathers arise—change comes.

The prophet Malachi declared that Elijah would come—not the literal man himself, but the Anointing of Elijah, to turn the hearts of the children to the Fathers (Malachi 4:6).

Some four hundred years later, the angel Gabriel brought God's message to Zacharias, father of John the Baptist. Gabriel did not use the term "children." Instead, he spoke of "the turning of the hearts of *the disobedient to the wisdom of the just*" (Luke 1:13–17). To us, his words may sound like a commentary on Malachi's prophecy, but in truth they were far more. It was God's own expanded unveiling on what had been spoken of before. *It was revealed Truth.*

God's children had strayed. Disobedient? Yes—otherwise it would not have been said. But how did they lose their way? What had caused them to go astray? What allowed the flames of devotion to dim? Looking closely at Malachi's prophecy alongside

angel Gabriel's message, we see two primary forces that stand exposed as the root causes:
- Fatherlessness crisis (a lack of Spirit-filled, Spirit-led fathering), and
- Lukewarmness (the chilling grip of a lukewarm spirit).

To begin with:
The word "children" in Malachi's prophecy refers to the sheep of the Church (mainly those who are not leaders or clergy in the Church). Viewed more broadly when we consider the Mantle of Elijah—which is a Revival Anointing—"children," in its proper context refers to all of God's sheep, His children. This aligns with the message delivered by the angel Gabriel, who added that the turning of the hearts would make ready a *people prepared for the Lord.*

Luke 1:16–17

(The angel Gabriel speaking)…And many of the children of Israel shall he (John) turn to the Lord their God. And he shall go before Him (Jesus) in the spirit and Power of Elias *(Elijah),* **to turn the hearts of the fathers to the children, and the disobedient to the wisdom of the just; to make ready a people prepared for the Lord.**

We can see here that the Spirit of the Lord, through Malachi and Gabriel, was addressing a deeper issue. I view prophetic messages much like fitting puzzle pieces together by asking the right questions. Why was there a need to cause the hearts of the *fathers to turn?* Was *the lack of fathering* thereof, the cause of the sheep's lukewarmness, and disobedience? I believe so. For if the sheep of God had gone astray, then what were the leaders—fathers of the Church doing, or failing to do, that allowed this to happen?

I remember a discussion about this in one of our ministry outings back in 2023. It was about lukewarmness and a fatherless generation. As I listened to the other ministers, I recalled a Word the Lord had given me a few years earlier, "A fatherless generation is the problem, and is the main reason for why the hearts of the children have turned away from Me. *The prodigals need a father that can call them home* (Luke 1:16–17)." I was deeply moved by this insight from the Holy Spirit. In that moment, the revelation unfolded before me. The prophet Malachi's words aligned with the angel Gabriel's message, and it all began to make sense in my spirit. If God was to turn the hearts of the *disobedient and lukewarm children* back to Him, He first had to turn the hearts of *the fathers* to Him. The root cause of this crisis is *fatherlessness*.

Repentance—the turning of hearts

The Lord Jesus abhors a lukewarm spirit. When addressing the Laodicean Church, He spoke with sharp authority, "Because you are lukewarm, I will spew you out of My Mouth... As many as I love, I rebuke and chasten: be zealous therefore, and *repent (be regretful and change your heart and mind or think differently)* (Revelation 3:15–17, 19)." In essence, Jesus was calling the Church to **turn her heart** in a new and radically different direction, to walk in zealous devotion once more.

"Repentance is the turning of hearts.

So, if "repentance" was what Gabriel was addressing, he made it clear that the Spirit and Power of Elijah—the Revival Mantle—will be the very cause and reason for this turning of hearts. That's a powerful statement worth repeating.

> "The Revival Mantle will be the very cause and reason for the turning of hearts.

Even religion, at its full strength, could not turn the hearts of the people to God. Outward works alone had no effect on the heart of man. In fact, all they accomplished was to keep the people bound to tradition and customs, causing them to *abandon* the weightier matters of the Word (Matthew 23:23).

So, when Jesus spoke to the Church to *repent,* He was already aware of their current trajectory and state of mind (Revelation 3:15). Their lukewarmness was drawing them away from Him, rather than toward Him. My fellow believers in the Lord, if lukewarmness characterises your life and mind, know this: it's leading you away from God.

There are only two main spiritual paths, each with its own end and distinct realities: righteousness that leads to eternal life through Christ Jesus; or sin and unbelief which lead to death (eternal damnation) (Matthew 25:46, Romans 6:23, Daniel 12:2). It is clear—Jesus desires for us to choose the path of righteousness in Him, the path that leads to eternal life (John 3:16).

> "God's part is to call you to repentance… Your part is to respond with a repentant heart. God cannot do your part for you. That decision is yours to make.

James 1:13–15

Let no man say when he is tempted, I am tempted of God: for God cannot be tempted with evil, neither tempteth He any man: But every man is tempted, when he is drawn away of his own lust, and enticed. Then when lust hath conceived, it bringeth forth sin: and sin, when it is finished, bringeth forth death.

Lukewarmness—Spiritual Adultery

Lukewarmness is spiritual complacency, negligence, rebelliousness and disobedience. If left unaddressed, its effects can cause great and irreparable damage. A person who lives a lukewarm life is like someone lying down on their side, right next to a poisonous snake. They see the snake, but they can't move quickly enough to free themselves. They are caught in a dilemma, double-minded about what to do.

If they attempt to move, the snake will strike before they even have the chance to escape. If they remain still, the snake will still strike anyway. It is already poised to strike and has drawn close enough to launch its attack. Picture for a moment that this person is you lying down on your side, with a poisonous snake within striking distance. It has locked eyes on you and is ready to attack… A serious matter, wouldn't you agree? The snake is merciless. It will not negotiate with you about your freedom. It has only one intent, and that is to destroy you.

Lukewarmness, as described in the illustration above, is also to be double-minded. The Greek word for "double-minded" is (dipsuchos). Which literally translates to "two-minded" or "two-souled." Lukewarmness is to be friends with the world while attempting to maintain a relationship with God. That is spiritual adultery.

James 4:4

Ye adulterers and adulteresses, know ye not that the friendship of the world is enmity with God?

Whosoever therefore will be a friend of the world is the enemy of God.

A lukewarm spirit is easily offended when confronted about its waywardness and sinfulness. If the Truth offends you, that means you have pride in your heart and you still love the world more than the Truth of God. For the person who entertains a lukewarm life, that lukewarmness, combined with offence, will keep that person bound and will even remain a stubborn *stumbling block* in their life.

James 4:6–10

But He giveth more grace. Wherefore He saith, God resisteth the proud, but giveth grace unto the humble. Submit yourselves therefore to God. Resist the devil, and he will flee from you. Draw nigh to God, and He will draw nigh to you. Cleanse your hands, ye sinners; and purify your hearts, ye double minded. Be afflicted, and mourn, and weep: let your laughter be turned to mourning, and your joy to heaviness. Humble yourselves in the sight of the Lord, and he shall lift you up.

Let's delve deeper and do a bit of analysing and interpreting. What you will see here is where this ends up (it's quite eye-opening):

Lukewarmness is a lack of concern—
- *Apathetic* (showing, or feeling no interest or concern),
- *Half-hearted* (without enthusiasm, or showing a lack of commitment).

Lukewarmness leads to negligence—

This lack of interest and concern then leads to *negligence and carelessness,* which is a failure to give enough (or proper) care to someone or something that you are responsible for.

The effects or results of negligence are:
- *Inattention and distractions* (lack of attention to duty/responsibility),
- *Dereliction* (a state of abandonment and becoming ruined),
- *Detached and disengaged* (emotionally and spiritually disconnected and separated). SPIRITUAL DRYNESS.

Lukewarmness breeds lawlessness and disobedience

Negligence then leads to *apostasy and lawlessness*:
- *Apostasy* (abandoning the Faith—no longer a true disciple and follower),
- *Lawlessness and Rebelliousness* (having no respect for laws, disobedient, and not governed by rules, standards, or laws).

In summary, a lukewarm spirit and culture lead to an unconcerned, negligent, lawless and disobedient life. Make no mistake. This is no minor issue—lukewarmness is not merely *borderline* Christianity; it is a deliberate choice to maintain a relationship with sin.

Isaiah 53:6

All we like sheep have gone astray; we have turned every one to his own way…

The apostle Peter described this lukewarm spirit as one "…having eyes full of adultery, and cannot cease from sin; beguiling unstable souls: hearts that exercise covetous practices; *cursed children*…who have forsaken the right way and have gone astray, loving the ways of unrighteousness (2 Peter 2:14–15)."

The apostle Paul addressed this same spirit, calling it "...a reprobate mind (immoral and corrupt), who doesn't retain God in his knowledge...being filled with all unrighteousness, fornication, wickedness, covetousness, maliciousness; full of envy, murder, debate, deceit, malignity (bitter and hostile); whisperers (talebearers), backbiters (slanderers), haters of God, despiteful, proud, boasters, inventors of evil things, *disobedient to parents* (Romans 1:28-30)." But for those who live and walk in Christ, *you are not reprobates. You are called to holiness and righteousness. Set apart by the Spirit of God.*

2 Corinthians 13:4–6
For though He (Jesus) was crucified through weakness, yet He liveth by the Power of God. For we also are weak in Him, but we shall live with Him by the Power of God toward you. Examine yourselves, whether ye be in the Faith; prove your own selves. Know ye not your own selves, how that Jesus Christ is in you, except ye be reprobates?...We are not reprobates

From this brief lexicological and biblical study of the meaning and behaviour of the word "lukewarm", it becomes clear that neglecting our walk with the Holy Spirit and rejecting Revival Culture opens the door to a spirit of lukewarmness and rebelliousness. We should be deeply concerned about this—because a lukewarm culture is the breeding ground for a lawless (ungodly) culture, eroding the very foundations of God's intended order.

In 2 Corinthians 13:4–6, Paul is not denying the fact that *we are weak*. No—he fully acknowledges it. But he doesn't leave it there. As I see it, what Paul is emphasising is that *our dependency on Christ and in His Power is the key to walking faithfully with Him*. We must trust in His leadership, regardless of our shortcomings, for the

Spirit of God will guide our steps and show us the way. Therefore, we are not to accept a reprobate life or mind—it was already crucified with Christ. For we have become *new in Him* (2 Corinthians 5:16–17, Colossians 1:21).

The Crisis of Fathering—Where Are the Fathers of Fire?

A lack of Spirit-inspired and Spirit-led mentorship is the glaring wound right now in the Church. It's not that we don't have fathers, but that we need fathers who are actively pursuing God's Heart— and God's Heart is to give us His Revival Fire. We don't just need leaders; we need Spirit-filled, Spirit-led fathers to rise up once again.

We are in a fatherlessness crisis. By fatherless, I do not only mean without a father; I mean, lacking the right kind of father— one who leads rightly and faithfully pursues his spiritual responsibilities in aligning with the Revival Mandate of God. I also refer to sons and daughters, who are unwilling to be mentored by a father. This is the *orphan spirit*. A person like this, in most cases, usually carries a wounded heart, always striving and never resting.

Whichever way you look at it, fatherlessness is the cause of lukewarmness and lawlessness—all these are the work of a spirit of disobedience and rebelliousness (Ephesians 2:1–3). The gaping wound created by this crisis of fatherlessness must be addressed without delay.

The truth is undeniable: God's people desperately need His Revival Anointing, combined with fathering that is led by the Holy Spirit. Only a Spirit-filled, Spirit-led life carries the Power to break the stronghold of a sin-driven culture (Isaiah 61:1, Zechariah 4:6–7). But when fathers fail to earnestly pursue God's Glory, they downplay its importance in the Church. Even worse, the sheep will absorb and adopt this spiritual apathy, calling it "normal." This is a cunning, insidious strategy of the enemy—working relentlessly through casual, lukewarm Christianity to keep God's people weak, defeated, distracted, and far from His Glory.

I must admit, I felt somewhat perplexed when I listened to ministers who claimed that the Power of God had been so wonderful in their meeting, yet when I looked for a demonstration of the Holy Spirit, I saw none. I understand that some ministers may feel inclined to defend their Church's liturgy, but the truth is this: programs are not a replacement for the Power of God's Presence.

Pastors, the sheep don't need religious routines; they need the Fire of God to grab hold of their hearts and lead them back to Jesus. Not only that, the Fire of God will keep them steadfast in their walk with Him, for He is the Word that illuminates our path (Psalms 119:105). As God's ministers, we must be concerned about the nurturing we are providing God's people. We can't expect them to know the ways of the Spirit if we aren't demonstrating the Spirit-filled life to them.

And let me add, there is a profound connection between *godly living and spiritual fathers*. As I mentioned earlier, many are currently lost in a sin-driven culture, walking with corrupted minds. I believe the primary reason is the lack of endorsement and engagement of Holy Spirit-led fathers—fathers who can rebuke, correct, instruct, inspire, equip and lead the sheep in the paths of Glory and righteousness.

Israel's king, Ahab, provides a striking example of a father who had walked away from the Lord. He was not only lukewarm but completely lawless. His heart was given to the worship of Baal, while still attempting to give half-hearted honour to *Yahweh*. Because of his leadership choices, the people interpreted his compromise as permission to go astray, and they too worshipped Baal.

Lukewarmness, Fatherlessness Crisis, & the Turning of Hearts   CHAPTER 16

This note is worth considering:
If you are a leader of the Church, I encourage you to reflect on this... In your next worship meeting, be the example of what authentic worship should look like. When you demonstrate it to the people of God, you are also giving them permission to adopt the posture of authentic worship. Their freedom of expression flows from your freedom of expression, because you lead the way. Your worship posture becomes their worship posture. If you are free, they are free (1 Corinthians 2:1–5).

And when we let the sheep of God encounter the Lord for themselves—in moments of breakthrough worship—we are building strong believers who want to be taught and led by the Lord. Leaders, understand this: you are not only pastoring their actions—you are doing more than that. You are pastoring their hearts, their minds, their likely decisions, their moments of testing and tribulation, their call, their growth and their directions. You are their leader, not just on the pulpit on Sunday, but all the time. They might not see you during the week, but they are aware that you are one who continually meets with God. I encourage you: let your private life with God be the impact and inspiration they need. If the turning of hearts is to happen, the sheep must have an example to follow. They need it not tomorrow, but now, and every single day.

A leadership that nurtures a Spirit-filled people is a leadership willing to journey from Glory to Glory with the Holy Spirit. Only a fathering heart, saturated with Spirit-led thoughts, can carry such a depth of mentorship. For our leadership must always point to *the Father's Heart*. We are called to mentor the sheep, not only with words, but also with deeds. As we lead a Spirit-filled life—in the steadfastness of the Anointing resting upon us—we become the very vessels through which God uses to turn many hearts toward Him. Even now, while you are on your knees before the Lord, you are ministering to them. The Power and influence of the Holy Spirit in your worship posture carries far more impact on others than you may realise. You are that shining city set upon a hill, placed there for such a time as this. You are God's lighthouse, guiding them to find their way.

> "The turning of hearts demands fathers of Fire. Revival demands fathers of Fire.

I conclude this chapter with a challenge for you: *the turning of hearts must happen.* But the question remains—will you be the vessel God will use to bring it about? If the sons are to turn their hearts and pursue God rightly, they need Holy-Spirit-filled and Holy-Spirit-led fathers to imitate and follow. As a spiritual father, if you're not pursuing the Holy Spirit, then you're failing your spiritual sons, and you are therefore not aligned to the Revival Mandate of God.

Prayer:
Dear Lord Jesus. We ask You to forgive us for not taking seriously the issues of lukewarmness and fatherlessness. Help us Lord. to return to that place You have chosen for us. That we may be filled with Your Spirit, and led by Your Spirit. In Jesus' Name, Amen.

May the Lord give your Revival Fathers who Not Only Walk in the Way of the Spirit, but Are Mandated to Teach You His Ways!

Lukewarmness, Fatherlessness Crisis, & the Turning of Hearts   CHAPTER 16

'When sons learn to walk with their Spirit-led fathers, they catch the heart and posture of how to walk with God.'

CHAPTER 17

Spirit-led Fathers Raise Spirit-led Sons

Imitate a father who follows Christ and is led by the Spirit.

Many ministers are skilled at preaching—they teach, instruct, and expound the Word—but few grasp the deeper responsibility of mentoring and fathering in the Holy Ghost. To be a Revivalist of God is not simply to lead and instruct; it is first and foremost to be a father in the House of God, standing as a beacon—a reflection of the Mind and Heart of Christ before His people. True fathering carries both prophetic guidance and apostolic authority, impacting lives through Holy-Spirit-led mentoring, by modelling the true worship posture without fear, by hosting the Presence of God, and through the impartation of Revival Knowledge.

1 Corinthians 4:14–16

> I write not these things to shame you, but as my beloved sons I warn you. For though ye have ten thousand instructors in Christ, yet have ye not many

fathers: for in Christ Jesus I have begotten you through the Gospel. Wherefore I beseech you, be ye followers of me.

1 Corinthians 11:1
Be ye followers of me, even as I also am of Christ.

Spirit-filled, Spirit-led fathers do more than teach—they prepare and mentor *willing sons to carry the Fire of God's Move.* They model how to *carry, lead, and serve* the Move of God with humility and Spirit-inspired confidence. Fathers who walk in Divine *encounters* raise sons who hunger for God encounters. Fathers who carry the prophetic burden and vision of the Move of God raise sons who are receptive and desire to carry the same Mantle of the Move of God —to run in step with the Spirit, with God's breakthrough Anointing operating in and through them. Thus, as fathers walk in the Presence and model lives lived in the flames of the Holy Ghost, each encounter overflows with His Power—passed to their sons as a living heritage of Glory.

> ### REVIVAL TRUTH:
> " The Revivalist of God, is firstly a father in the House of God, representing and upholding the Mind and Heart of Christ before the people.

From Father to Son: An Inheritance of Glory Encounters:

Isaac encountered the Living God by walking with his father, Abraham. At Mount Moriah, it was a sacrifice that met encounter—

where man's heart met God's Heart. Abraham's obedience was not just plain obedience; it was obedience that accessed the God-realm and made provision for something far greater than the natural realm. When God wants to do something great, He always pursues a man who pursues His Heart.

Abraham's heart must have been broken for his son. The pain of this sacrifice positioned Abraham to receive a Divine Reward that would last for eternity, and Isaac had the blessing of being a part of it. At Mount Moriah, Isaac experienced both pain and redemption. He experienced the faith of His father, and the Favour of the FATHER. He had the blessing of encountering not just God, but *God's Heart*. (For while he lay on the altar, he would have heard everything the angel said to his father—Genesis 22).

Many years later, Isaac passed this peculiar blessing to Jacob—an *open-heaven life,* open to God encounters (Genesis 28:7–22). Then Jacob had his opportunity to meet God at *Bethel—The House of God.* What Jacob didn't fully understand was that the Covenant-keeping God wanted him *to see and hear the God-realm.* God desired Jacob's heart, just as He had desired Abraham's and Isaac's heart.

Later, Jacob did the same and passed this inheritance of God encounters to his sons (Genesis 35:1-15). Nothing is ordinary when Heaven invades Earth. Nothing is ordinary when the Heavenly realm becomes available to man. When ABBA FATHER wants an audience with man, it is Glory touching the earth.

About 430 years later from Abraham, when the Lord spoke to Moses from the Burning Bush (Exodus 3-4), He introduced Himself as the God of Abraham, Isaac and Jacob.

Exodus 3:14–15

And God said unto Moses, I AM THAT I AM: and He said, "Thus shalt thou say unto the children of Israel, I AM hath sent me unto you." And God said moreover unto Moses, "Thus shalt thou say unto the children of Israel, The LORD God of your fathers, the God of Abraham, the God of Isaac, and the God of Jacob, hath sent me unto you: this is My Name for ever, and this is My Memorial unto all generations."

Whether Moses realised it or not, as the Lord talked with him, the Fire of God's Words descended upon him, igniting a Mandate for the Exodus of God's people. Moses was commissioned in holy conversation with the Living God, and God's Words rested on him as the Mantle to bring Israel out of bondage.

"God-encounters lead to God-initiated Revival.

Exodus means a mass departure of a people. And the work of Revival is exactly that—a mass departure from bondage and idolatry. But an exodus can only happen when *a Fire-carrying messenger* brings the Power of God's Word to the people.

Additionally, the Revival Mandate is not only to do with departure from bondage but also about entering into and possessing *a Promise*. Thus, the Church must go beyond merely breaking free from bondage and adopt a strong, determined posture to pursue the abiding of the Glory—that is our inheritance.

When Moses took up this call at the age of eighty and came to deliver Israel from Egypt, he quickly caught the attention of a young Joshua, who was about forty years old. Joshua was captivated by *the Power of Yahweh working through Moses*. Here, we see an important principle: Joshua exemplified it—*spiritual sons need to see before they can follow*. Thus, the Holy Spirit's *demonstration working through a spiritual father* allows sons to capture the Move, and to receive their appointed Mantle.

"Demonstration is Revival Language.

Spiritual sons only *catch the Move* when their spiritual fathers demonstrate it correctly, with trembling and sincerity in their hearts. Moses approached his calling with a similar kind of trembling, as the apostle Paul later described (1 Corinthians 2:1–5), for the *weight of God's Mandate rested heavily upon him.* Thus, Joshua witnessed both the Power of God demonstrated through Moses and the trembling posture of the mantled vessel.

> **1 Corinthians 2:1–5**
> And I, brethren, when I came to you, came not with excellency of speech or of wisdom, declaring unto you the testimony of God. For I determined not to know any thing among you, save Jesus Christ, and Him crucified. And I was with you in weakness, and in fear, and in much trembling. And my speech and my preaching was not with enticing words of man's wisdom, but in demonstration of the Spirit and of Power: That your faith should not stand in the wisdom of men, but in the Power of God.

Spirit-led Fathers Are the Key to Raising Spirit-led Sons

Spirit-led fathers are the key to raising Spirit-led sons. In the Move of God, there can be no lesser standard than fathers who are both Spirit-filled and Spirit-led. There are the fathers who carry the Mandate and impart it to their sons. And when a generation rises with a holy hunger for the Move of God, it is the undeniable evidence that true spiritual fathers have stirred the flames of passion for the Glory to move in their midst.

A related note:
Revivalists-fathers walk together in the oneness of heart. They understand that the unity of the fathers produces the unity of the sons. With this awareness, they impart Kingdom principles to their spiritual sons, knowing that the unity of the sons will strengthen and encourage the unity of the generation that follows.

A father of the Move is one who relentlessly pursues Christ and the Mandate of the Move of God. He has made God's Desire his desire, and He pursues what God pursues. Yet, if fathers grow casual in their posture before God, they will drift from the Fire, and become void of the effectiveness and tangibleness of the Mantle entrusted to them.

A true spiritual father doesn't merely gather followers—he raises leaders. He seeks three qualities in his spiritual sons: *their full attention, their willing obedience, and their humility of heart.* These were the very traits found in Joshua. *Diligent fathers raise diligent sons—*that's the impact of proper mentorship reproduced in true sons. Yet this principle rests on one condition: it works only with *willing sons,* whose hearts are aligned to their father's heart, until his pursuit becomes their pursuit.

Holy Ghost-led, God-called fathers are more than just fathers—they are mentors, shepherds, and confident leaders in the things of the Spirit. They are mighty men in the things of the spirit realm, men of renown in the heavenlies because their prayer life, and their anointed, passionate mentoring have shaped the destinies of many. Humble and yielded, they move in step with the Spirit. This kind of *fathering* is caught by willing sons who have observed the ways of their fathers and have learnt how to walk as *responsible* Spirit-filled, Spirit-led vessels. From their fathers, they have discovered how to be *carriers, leaders and servants* of the Great Divine Revival Mandate. They have matured with deep wells of Divine counsel, and their Mantle is powerful because they have learnt how to *honour the Anointing of the Revivalist.*

This is the very model imparted by the Lord Jesus to His disciples. When they came under the baptism of Fire in the Upper Room, they were transformed into powerful leaders of the Move of God.

A Note to the Sons

True Spirit-led fathers disciple sons into the Christ-like Life and the Christ-like Mind. They lead them in *the deep things of the Move of God*. When a father is carrying a Revival Mantle, his desire is that his sons pursue God alongside him. This is a sacred and unique proposition for sons: a Divine vocation, established by the Holy Spirit. It is no ordinary place in the realms of the spirit. A father who walks with God occupies a rare place, and only steadfast, unwavering sons will desire to walk in it.

So they must first be *willing* sons—ready to walk where their father walks, to persist with a kind of passion that wants to grab something from their father. They must want to see what he sees and to hear the Heart of God as He hears. They must want God for themselves as they seek a personal encounter with the Living God.

A true son must have the right heart posture to go through the moulding of Revival Mentorship. For only then can he become a Glory Carrier. When a son aligns his heart to his father's pursuit, he catches the Fire of the Mantle carried by his father. Catching the Mantle is no small matter. The Mantle's influence is impactful and life-changing. When a son has walked like his father, this son will eventually also be endowed with a mighty Mantle and become a great father and mentor to many sons.

A spiritual son's heart posture will determine his ability to catch the Move, beginning with learning to honour the Spirit of the

Move. He must first humble himself before the God of all Anointings and desire intimacy with God. Again, *he must observe the way of his Spirit-led, Spirit-filled fathers before he can follow.*

Keep your eyes on a son who is diligent in God's business; he shall stand before great men and be recognised (Proverbs 22:29). Sons, if you are diligent with the same heart attitude as your spiritual father, the Lord will open doors before you, and the mantle of leadership and Divine responsibility will rest upon you.

Spirit-filled fathers also honour *the uniqueness* of their sons. They work with what God is shaping in each vessel, knowing that every Anointing operates uniquely through the one who carries it. Sons must, however, guard against a pseudo mindset. A son wanting to be like his father must be careful not to be pretentious by mimicking his father, for the Anointing cannot be mimicked—it is only caught and imparted. The goal, therefore, is for a son to remain authentic and unique while faithfully pursuing the things of God. And when God sees that the son is ready to receive His special Mantle, it will be given to him.

Not contradicting this statement but further validating it: a son may, on occasions, *sound a bit like his spiritual father*. This manifestly shows that the son has been walking closely with his father, and varying aspects of the father's knowledge, understanding, and *Mantle-traits* have been imparted to him. This is the fruit of genuine Holy Spirit mentorship—it is not forced; it is *imparted by the Grace and Power of the Spirit*.

It is not the father who is exalted here, but the Spirit of Christ at work in the father, now fully functioning in the son. The apostle Paul expressed it this way, "Be ye followers of me, even as I also am of Christ" (1 Corinthians 11:1). Paul wasn't demanding mere following; he was laying down a Kingdom Truth that, if observed correctly, would bring a great blessing to the Body of Christ.

I agree with Paul and strongly exhort the same principle concerning holy mentorship for the Move: *follow a Spirit-filled,*

Spirit-led leader who follows Christ and points you to Christ. When you practice this pursuit, you will catch the Move, and you too will be endowed with a powerful Revival Mantle.

An example of this is the evangelist Philip, who was mightily used by God. He was not an apostle, yet he pursued what his spiritual fathers pursued. The Book of Acts does not state whether he was one of the hundred and twenty saints in the Upper Room, but it does record that he was one of the seven Spirit-filled individuals chosen to serve tables. When you serve willingly, you demonstrate the correct heart attitude and position yourself as one ready to be used for the Glory of God.

Joshua & Seymour: Sons Who Caught the Move of God

A powerful example of a spiritual father—son relationship is seen between Moses and Joshua. Joshua served faithfully as Moses' minister—a true spiritual son who was willing to serve the weight of the Mandate that rested on his father: to be led by the Glory of God. This special Anointing to *carry the Move,* so deeply captivated Joshua's heart that it shaped the course of his life. Over the long years in the wilderness, Joshua learnt how to walk with God, not merely by instruction, but by closely observing Moses, who dwelt continually in the Presence.

There is something powerful about serving the Anointing. It is through a posture of humility and proximity that a son becomes familiar with the Anointing. In that closeness, he learns to discern and recognise unique traits of the Anointing and how it operates through a vessel chosen by God.

"The heart that discerns the Anointing will also recognise the Power of God at work through that Anointing.

When you not only recognise the Anointing but also serve the one who carries it, you position yourself to receive a powerful blessing from the God of the Great Revival Mandate. The Anointing you serve opens access to the very blessings that Anointing contains. Yet, we must note an important distinction: there is a difference between being close to the servant of God and being close to the Mantle he carries. Many can linger within the circles of a servant of God, but only a few—led by the Spirit—are drawn to serve the weight of the Mantle upon his life.

A note of caution to the Mantle Wearer:
To those who wear a Revival Mantle and have become fathers of the Move: God will indeed assign sons to serve the Mantle you wear, but never abuse this holy privilege. How we treat others matters deeply. We must walk reverently, humbly and tenderly with Grace and Truth—for the Mantle is a holy trust. Honour the Mantle, but also honour God's people—for they are the very reason the Mantle was given. As Mantle Wearers, we are called to serve God's Mandate to His people, representing Christ faithfully and correctly before them at all times. And when you find a son who longs for what you carry, do not keep him at a distance—draw him close.

Joshua sat under the blessed Anointing given to Moses. His heart was perfectly aligned with his father's heart. Amazingly, Joshua served the Revival Mandate upon Moses's life for forty years, and Moses never stopped Joshua from pursuing God.

When Moses was with God forty days and forty nights in the Glory Cloud, Joshua was right there sitting in proximity to the Cloud. Joshua didn't think it unfair to sit outside of the Glory Cloud—to him, it was enough to sit at the doorway of this amazing experience (Exodus 32:13–18).

This reminds me of another prominent Revivalist who understood this holy blessing: William Seymour, the Catalyst and Carrier of the Azusa Street Revival (1906-1915). Because of Jim Crow Segregation Laws.[11-12] Seymour, being coloured, wasn't allowed in the classroom with white students. But his spiritual father, Charles Parham, made sure he wouldn't miss out. He made provision for Seymour to sit outside in the hallway, near the open door of the room.

This did not deter Seymour, nor did it cause offence. Because he had the right heart attitude, it was enough for him to have *the special privilege* of sitting at the doorway of the supernatural Word. He gleaned with deep consciousness and soaked in every word, every lesson, and every drop of Divine wisdom flowing from that room.

Outwardly, this segregation might seem unjust, even discouraging—and you might even feel sorry for Seymour. But don't judge by the natural view of things. Something far more profound and glorious had gripped his heart. In reality, Seymour was already seated at the abundant Table of the King of Glory. The sweetness of the Move of God was already working in him, this humble son, who didn't yet know that he would later become the very instrument God would use to release Revival Fire to the nations.

What a marvellous story to tell. It is more than a testimony of resilience—it is a testimony of pure hunger and love for the Move of God. It was this son, who sat in proximity to the Glory of the Word, who later became the Carrier of one of the greatest Moves in the Church's history. The segregation of coloureds and whites in those days did not, for a moment, hinder this *holy progress* working in Seymour's spirit.

The mighty Revivalist-Pastor, William Seymour, stands as our example of the attitude and posture that *catches and carries the Revival Fire.*

Friends, I can share with you these Revival Truths, but *Revival can only be caught by a humble and honouring heart.* Position yourselves at the doorway of God's Glory, lean close to the flow of His Word, and wait with hearts ready to receive the Fire that will shake the nations!

Prayer:

Mighty God, Everlasting Father, we thank you for giving us spiritual fathers. You are our Father, and the Shepherd of our souls. Lead us to Your great and glorious Move—for we are ready and willing to follow. In Jesus' Name, Amen...

May the Mantle of the Move Rest Mightily Upon You!

ENDNOTES:

11.   Laurie KleinCecil M. Robeck Jr., The Azusa Street Mission and Revival: The Birth of the Global Pentecostal Movement (Nashville: Thomas Nelson, 2006), 41–43.

12.   Vinson Synan, The Holiness-Pentecostal Tradition: Charismatic Movements in the Twentieth Century (Grand Rapids: Eerdmans Publishing, 1997), 103–105.

CHAPTER 17

Part 8 – Reclaiming the Fire of the Upper Room

'Revival Fire resting upon the Church is Power with God.'

CHAPTER 18

Leaders of Babel vs. Leaders of the Upper Room

Powerlessness in the Church is unacceptable.

I want to compare two leadership models that operate in the Church—Babel versus Upper Room. One is earthly, driven by human-led efforts and human-centred insights. The other is of the Spirit, established through Spirit-led initiatives and Spirit-level revelation.

Listen carefully: it is dangerous to raise a Church without Spirit-led, Spirit-inspired initiatives. Revival is not built by good intentions alone—it is a Holy-Spirit-led movement. Even with the best intentions, without the Holy Spirit guiding every step, you risk building God's work like Babel, reaching high in human effort but lacking the depth and substance of true Holy-Spirit leadership. The result? People who are spiritually malnourished, starving for the Bread of the Holy Ghost.

The apostles and prophets were Spirit-led, Spirit-filled individuals. If the foundations of the Church were laid by them, then every structure, every framework, and every initiative that follows must flow from that Spirit-led order—*as is fitting for a Spirit-led, Spirit-filled people called to carry His Glory.*

Ephesians 2:18–22

For through Him we both have access by one Spirit unto the Father. Now therefore ye are no more strangers and foreigners, but fellowcitizens with the saints, and of the household of God; And are built upon the foundation of the apostles and prophets, Jesus Christ himself being the Chief Corner Stone; In whom all the building fitly framed together groweth unto an Holy Temple in the Lord: In whom ye also are **builded together for an Habitation of God through the Spirit.**

Pastors, whether you realise this or not, when you forget the ways of the Upper Room, you lose sight of *the posture that hosts the Glory.* Don't get me wrong, human effort has its place but it can never replace the Power that the Church is meant to host and operate in. All too often, we attempt to exclude God from *His own Move,* believing that our efforts, as the main component of ministry, will accomplish Divine exploits. In doing so, we miss the vital life source of the Spirit—the Power that quickens our spirits. If God chooses to work in a certain way, it is always for His Glory—not ours.

At Babel, human-led efforts pursue a direction that doesn't run alongside the Spirit—it's not even close. The Upper Room, on the other hand, reflects a completely different mindset and purpose. It was Holy-Spirit-initiated and Holy-Spirit-led. God was leading *the Cause for the Move,* and He was leading hearts.

Babel reveals man's ambitions and is the inverse of the mindset and heart-attitude that hosts the Glory. While intentions may be well-meaning, they are not necessarily Spirit-led or Spirit-inspired. The two paths—Babel and the Upper Room—run entirely in two different directions. The Upper Room reveals God's Heart to be in the midst of His people, firmly rooted in the way the Spirit moves. It is no wonder that God shook and dismantled Babel, yet *empowered and mantled the Upper Room with His Glory.*

At Babel, mankind sought to build a kingdom up to God. It was not to glorify God, but to make a name for themselves (Genesis 11:4). In contrast, the Upper Room, God brought His Kingdom down to man, and He was exalted in their midst. This Baptism of Fire empowered the disciples to go forth and proclaim the Name of Jesus—bringing glory to God, not to man.

I encourage each believer to be led by the Spirit—to walk as individuals guided and inspired by the Holy Ghost. We must never, not even for a moment, assume that our efforts are sufficient. In reality, we are only touching the surface of what is hidden in God.

Let us take to heart King Solomon's counsel: "Trust in the Lord with all your heart and lean not on your own understanding; in all your ways, acknowledge Him, and He shall direct your path" (Proverbs 3:5-6). As we pursue God and acknowledge Him as the Leader and Chief Apostle of our Calling and Ministry, we remain hidden in Him. And in due time, we shall be revealed by the Power of His Spirit resting on us.

Unity that Hosts the Glory

Babel had unity, but God was not part of that unity (Genesis 6:11). The Upper Room's oneness, however, was of a different kind —it was unity in the Holy Ghost (Acts 2:1). Oneness with the Holy

Ghost is a powerful reality. It resounds with what the Psalmist proclaimed in Psalms 133, that where the Anointing Oil pours *like dew from Heaven, there the Lord commands the Blessing*. It was the Glory that settled like *dew* upon the hundred and twenty disciples, thoroughly baptising them with God's Power. In that holy moment, the *shoes of earthly reputation and human confidence gave way to Holy Ground of encounter. The Fire of the Spirit had come and God spoke there again so powerfully that He flowed like rivers from out of their innermost being* (John 7:38). That not-so-significant, seemingly ordinary room, became holy grounds because of the Glory.

> "To walk in God and with God is to be in agreement with the Holy Spirit.

Liberty in the Spirit comes from the oneness of hearts—and this releases faith to grasp the moving of the Spirit in the room. *Unity is a matter of the heart.* It's one thing to pray for unity in the Body of Christ; it's another thing entirely to live and *represent* the message of unity, even toward those who may offend you. Unity is to have our hearts in AGREEMENT (Acts 2:1).

> **REVIVAL TRUTH:**
>
> " True Unity is a foundational part of 'the Knowledge' that hosts the Revival Blessing.

When Jesus said, "Where two or three are gathered in My Name," this is not merely a statement about numbers—it is a declaration about the posture of our hearts. True Revival flows where hearts are aligned (Matthew 20:33). When believers walk together in agreement, the spirit of division loses its foothold, and makes way for the Power of the Spirit of God.

Applied with understanding, we see that the greater Revival Blessing comes to those who advocate for and represent correctly the message of unity in the Body of Christ. If the Lord our God is ONE, then we too must be one—in Him (Ephesians 4:1–7).

A Man-led Church vs Authentic Worship

We must not fool ourselves. Powerlessness is not what God intended for His Church. Without the Fire of God, all that remains is form without Power: programs without Presence, and songs that stir the room but have no effect on the heart.

A man-led church may love the polished nature of its programs and treat sermons with an unshaken devotion to human effort, but nothing more. We can applaud services that showcase the excellence of man's ability to conduct worship, but if the Fire does not fall, it remains a barren Altar—and God is not there.

The tragedy is this: we've learned to gather without God. We've become a powerless people. We treat God as a monument to be venerated, rather than the Living Presence to be hosted in our midst. We've got it all wrong because we have built altars that serve talents and egos, platforms that elevate charisma, and monuments to personality. From these very stages, preachers speak of the Fire as a distant outcome, never realising that the Fire is already in their midst—waiting for someone to respond.

The groaning of intercession has been replaced with the excited pace of production. We've mastered the lighting of rooms, perfected the sound engineering, and even added fog machines to create an atmosphere—but none of these can attract the magnificent Glory of the Abiding Word.

All these efforts resemble those of the prophets of Baal on Mount Carmel. The man-led church cries louder and dances harder—yet there is no answer: no Fire, no Voice from Heaven.

PART 8   *Revival or Ruin: Reclaiming the Fire of the Upper Room*

> **REVIVAL TRUTH:**
>
> " The Sound of the Upper Room was the Sound of the Revival Fire (the Glory of God) resting upon the people.

But **there is an Altar that God recognises.** That Altar is the heart of true worshippers who have chosen to say "Yes" to the Anointing of the Spirit. They are not there for the crowd; they are there to host the Glory. No matter how good the music team sounds, God is not impressed by noise—He is drawn to a heart that wants the Power of His Presence. He responds to the authentic heart that knows how to receive and host His Glory. The noise of Babel was that of confusion. Conversely, the Sound of the Upper Room was that of *Revival Fire resting upon earthen vessels who aligned their hearts with God, and to the Revival Mandate.*

Now the Spirit of the Lord is once again asking: "Where is My Prepared Altar? Where is the Place of My Rest?"

I submit this to you: Revival will come where hearts are ready to receive Him. And the moment we step aside, yielding fully to His Presence—that's when the Fire is ready to Fall.

Reclaiming the Fire of the Upper Room

If the Church is to reclaim the Fire of the Upper Room, we must first return to *the Posture* that receives and hosts the Fire. The Upper Room is not just a historical account of the Church's birth—it is the story of *Heaven's most treasured Power placed in earthen vessels* (2 Corinthians 4:6–7). In that humble room, God's Move was ignited, and His Glory became tangible in their midst.

The Christ-redeemed man became *the new Altar, the new Living Temple, the New Ark of God*—a habitation of God through the Spirit

(Ephesians 2:22). *The Lord* would no longer need to seek for that identifying *mark* of the Glory-carrier, asking, "Where art thou?" And man would no longer fear the Voice of God (Genesis 3:9-10, John 14:17–18).

Therefore, we must return to that place. We must reclaim our place by embracing the posture that recognises the Glory. It is a posture of communion and surrender—the very posture that meets with God. Now is the time to enter this holy season of encounter. We are ordained for this.

For the Spirit desires that we pursue Him diligently and with passion, opening our hearts wide to receive more than we have ever imagined. Do not hesitate! Don't be afraid to go where He is calling! That place of holy encounter belongs to you—it has been predetermined by the Holy Spirit. We are called to encounter great things in the Holy Ghost. Now is the season to align and arise. Now is the time to step fully into His Glory. *Step into the Revival Fire!*

Prayer:

> Holy Spirit, we align our hearts to You. We say "Yes" to Your Revival Fire. We are ready to receive from You, oh Holy One. Cause us to hear Your Voice and be baptised in the Power of Your Presence. In Jesus' Name...Amen.

May the Spirit of Grace Rest Upon You and Prepare Your Hearts for the Day of the Great Awakening!

Part 9 – The Posture that Attracts, Hosts, & Releases the Glory

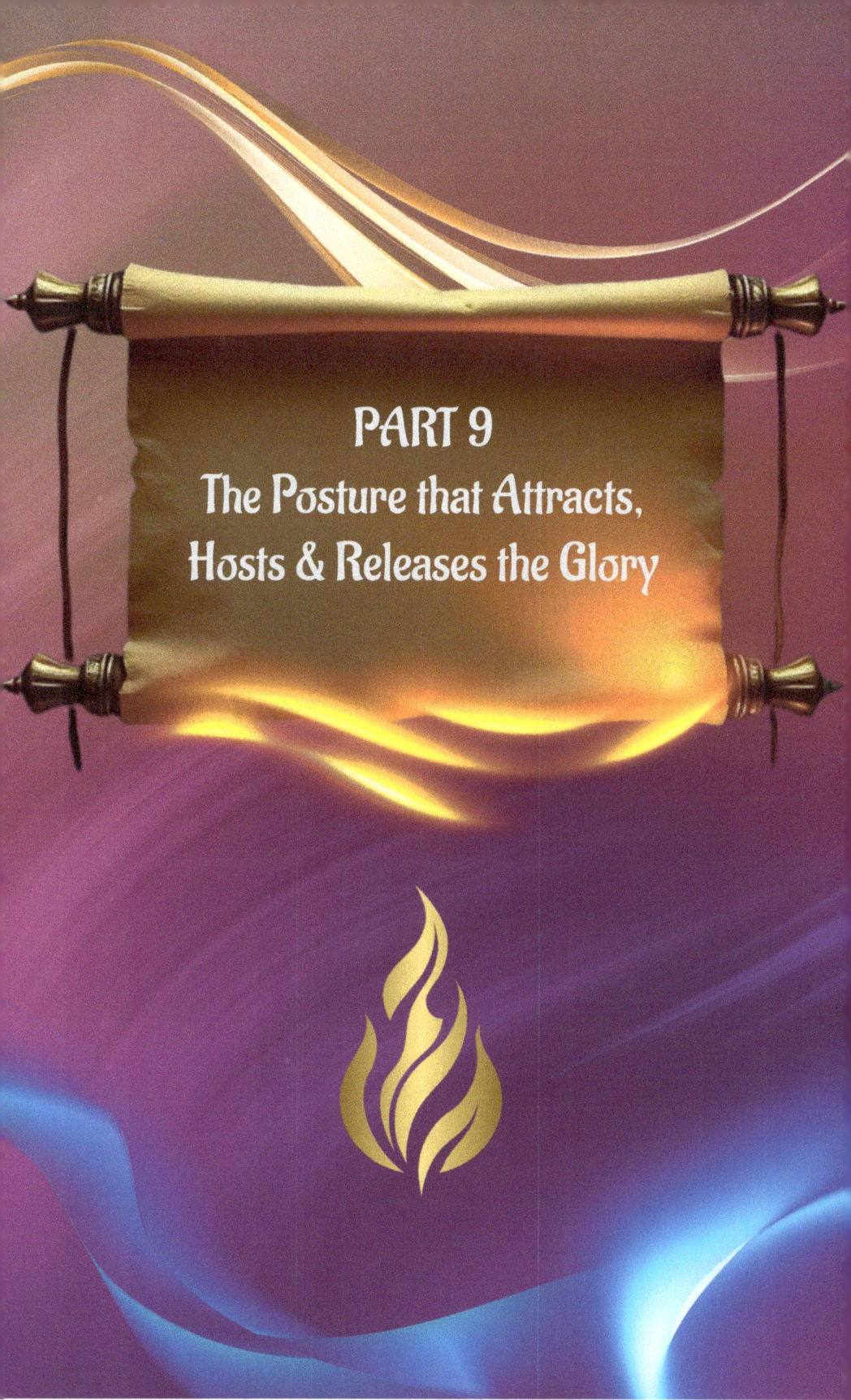

'Holy Spirit Standard:
THE ROD OF REVIVAL,
where the Power of God
merges with the Posture of
the Earthen Vessel'

CHAPTER 19

The Spirit of the Lord Shall Raise A Standard

The Holy Spirit's STANDARD will be initiated and carried by those who have raised the Rod of God's Revival as an ENSIGN to the Nations.

During a time of fellowship on the 3rd of May, 2024, I heard the Lord say to me, "Lift up My Rod of Revival, My servant. Lift up My Banner, My Moses." The Holy Spirit repeated this three times to me. At first, I thought, how can I lift up *the Rod of Revival,* seeing there is no rod in my hands? But then, as I waited on the Lord, I immediately understood that He was referring to *my worship posture.*

As plain as this Truth is, it is not easily understood and also difficult to make room for. This is largely because many clergy (or leaders) of the present-day Church have little or no revelation of the worship posture that *hosts* the Glory. Too often, I see ministers struggling to adopt a Spirit-and-in-Truth posture because they are so focused on the convenience of the meeting rather than adopting a posture for encounter with God. I see them lift their hands, but their hearts are struggling to be receptive because they're distracted by the desire for a perfect program. They are more devoted to the program than the Moving of the Spirit. Worse still, they often despise *rowdy worshippers* who don't fit their ideal worship style. As much as I would like to soften this, the truth remains: a lack of revelation about our worship is the root cause of this problem. But if you, oh minister, knew that to be broken before God is Power with Him, then God's Revival-work will be evident in you, and would shift the room mightily—for the Power of God speaks and leads at the same time.

And if we are to prostrate ourselves before Him, let it not be with boastfulness—for we have nothing to brag about before the Presence of God. Our brokenness before Him speaks louder than we realise. And the Glory responds when our hearts have come not to impress Him, but *to meet with Him*. It's worship that Moves Heaven and *hosts* the *manifestation and revelation* of the Word of Glory. The way of the *cleft of the Rock* demands this: that our heart meets with His Heart. For when you know His Heart, you will also know His Ways. And knowing Him is more than just a relationship —it is Authority and Power with God.

The Worship Posture: The *Nûs* & *Degel of God*

When Isaiah prophesied about the Glory of the Lord, he emphasised that the Spirit would lift up a mighty *Standard* against the enemy. Isaiah saw something deep and powerful in God. *"He beheld the Standard of the Spirit lifted up."* Yet, we can easily miss the weight of this passage—that the Glory which was to rest upon God's people (see Isaiah 60:1), came with a *Standard*. We should therefore ask, "What is that Standard?"

Isaiah 59:19

So shall they fear the Name of the LORD from the west, and His Glory from the rising of the sun. When the enemy shall come in like a flood, **the Spirit of the LORD shall lift up a 'Standard' against him.**

That *Standard is our worship posture*. But to better understand this Truth, we must first look at the prophecy I mentioned earlier about "Revival as the Rod of God." (I was blown away by this powerful revelation) The revelation about *the Standard* came quickly to my spirit as the Holy Spirit spoke to me. In a vision, I saw the prophet Moses standing with the wooden rod in his hands, lifted up over the battlefield. As I looked, my eyes were open to see its true meaning. I believe I saw what Isaiah saw.

A Divine instruction was given to Moses: to go and stand on a hill, facing the battlegrounds where the Amalekites had gathered to fight against Israel. Moses instructed Joshua to go forth and fight against the Amalekites, while he himself would stand on the hill to hold up *the Rod of God*. Moses was commanded to keep this posture until Joshua and the Israelites prevailed against the Amalekites and won the victory (Exodus 17:8–16; cf. Numbers 2:1-3). For as long as *the Rod was raised and held up by God's Chosen Vessel,* Israel prevailed in battle. Note here that God had not only secured victory over an earthly enemy, but over the demonic (spiritual) forces operating behind them, which stood against Israel. Thus, the *lifting up of the Rod* had a deeper spiritual purpose: the merging of *vessel and posture, with the Word of Glory and Power.*

Now, the Hebrew word which Isaiah used for "…lift up a Standard…" is *Nûs*, meaning:
- to cause to flee,
- to chase, or to deliver, and

- to lift up a standard (banner), and proclaim victory over the enemy.

The extent of this definition encompasses victories already won. It was *Divine Proclamation* not merely to be postured for battle, but to be postured to win the victory. When the enemy was defeated, *victory banners* were raised. We can understand this better by looking back into the history of wars and the significance of *ensigns* used by armies.

In ancient times, *flags* served not only as signals to guide troops in battle, but also as *powerful symbols* of identity, pride, confidence, and victory. These virtues and ethos have carried through to our present day. The armies of nations each have their *own Colours or Ensigns*.

A relevant note:

In military tradition, Colours (or Royal Ensigns) are flags that symbolise and embody the honour, values, ethos, culture, rich history, identity, and mandates of that military establishment. They are not merely banners, but are treated as sacred emblems of loyalty, honour, and sacrifice.

During my time in the Papua New Guinea Defence Force, I learned something very valuable about *the Colours or Royal Ensigns,* as they were called. These held a sacred status and were venerated as a powerful symbol of the regiment. The Colours were never allowed to be dropped or to touch the ground. They were kept in special places and were only handled by appointed soldiers, who were required to wear the proper ceremonial attire before carrying them. The Royal Ensigns were brought out only at appointed times, for special ceremonial parades, or in hosting dignitaries. Their significance was close to holy, so to speak. To lose the Colours in battle was historically considered the greatest dishonour—as if the very soul of the regiment had been taken. This would be akin to Israel losing the Ark of the Covenant to the Philistines (1 Samuel 4–5).

When we look at Numbers 2, we see God instructing the arrangement of the camp of Israel before the Glory Cloud. The Lord used the word *standard or flag* (in Hebrew, *Degel*) to mark the allocations.

Although not identical in meaning to *Nûs*, it fits within the overarching purpose of *a standard*. For example, when protestors take to the streets to *raise awareness* (to fight for their cause—*Nûs*), they *raise banners* (*Degel*) and shout messages to make their intentions known.

God intended that each banner (*Degel*) served as an *ensign* to represent each tribe and the way they were arrayed in their (army) divisions. Positioned in the centre of the camp were the Levites (the appointed priests, set apart to serve God and His ministry to the people). They too had a banner raised for them (Numbers 2:17).

In light of what we have just learnt about banners and their importance, we can now understand the significance of the instruction given to Moses. The man of God was to go up to the hill to raise *the Rod* as God's Ensign (*Degel*)—the symbol of His victory and power over the enemy (*Nûs*)—to put the enemy to flight. God was making a bold, Divine statement to the Amalekites. He was saying, "The battle belongs to Me (the Lord) before it even starts, and I will have victory over you (2 Chronicles 20:12–18)." God gave instructions to Moses that would ensure that victory was won. Hallelujah!

Consider this: that the outcome of this battle would be determined by Moses's obedience and posture. Israel's victory relied on his crucial part, and Moses needed to carry it out correctly. He was to ascend the hill and hold up *the Rod of God*. The moment Moses—the Chosen Leader of God—raised the holy Rod, it became *the Banner of the Lord: the Standard* lifted to declare victory over the enemy. In the same way, Revival Fire—and the posture that hosts the Fire—is God's Standard that will shake the nations.

And now, the Banner (*Degel*) of the Great Revival Mandate is ready to be raised to proclaim the Standard (*Nûs*) of the Lord. The *worship posture* of the Revivalist is *that Banner (Degel)* of God, which must be displayed. For it is *the Standard that proclaims victory* (*Nûs*) over the enemy.

Obedience is worship, and worship is also a weapon of warfare that puts the enemy to flight. There's more to your worship posture than you realise. That powerful act of humbling your heart before God is the very thing God will use to raise the Standard against the enemy and put the enemy to flight. Like the Rod in Moses's hands, your worship represents and proclaims:

- Your assigned Anointing and Mandate;
- That you are marked by the Holy Spirit to be used for His Glory;
- Your obedience and heart before the Lord, and
- God's (banner of) victory over the enemy

Your worship posture is the *Degel (ensign)* of God's Revival Mandate proclaiming *(Nûs)* victory over the enemy. In addition, the rugged *wooden Rod* reflects us as earthen vessels. None of us are perfect and none of us deserve to be used by the Lord. Yet, it is God's good pleasure to use us to bring about the fulfilment of His plans and to bring glory to His Name.

It's a powerful testimony that, as Moses raised the wooden Rod (the *Degel*), he was beholding *Yahweh Nissi*. This is such a crucial revelation for us also. *To behold the Word of Glory is to receive the Blessed Revival!* And our worship *posture is the very thing that allows us to behold God*. Hallelujah! Our part is the posture, and God's part is the Revival Fire.

Delving deeper into our discussion…after the Israelites had won the victory over their enemy, Moses *built an Altar* to the Lord upon that very hill where he had raised the Rod, and named the Altar *"Yahweh Nissi"*—The Lord my *Banner* (Exodus 17:15). The word, *Nissi* is derived from the word *Nês* (pronunciation: Nace) meaning a banner, pole, flagstaff, or sign.

This same word *Nês,* is used again when Moses made a fiery serpent and lifted it upon a *pole* (*Nês*) (Numbers 21:5–9). Everyone who had been bitten by poisonous snakes, when they looked upon the *Nês*—*serpent* that became the curse for them—was healed. Amazing, isn't it? This very event was a foreshadowing of the crucifixion of Christ. Just as the *Nês carried* the curse of the people and brought them healing, so also did our Lord Jesus Christ when He became that cursed *pole* (*Nês*) for us on the Cross. As it is written, "By His wounds we are healed (Isaiah 53:5)."

I reflect deeply that while Christ hung on the Cross for us, He not only brought healing but also secured the ultimate victory over every spiritual enemy—sin, death, demonic principalities and rulers, and hell itself (John 16:33). Through the Cross, Christ became the *Nês* lifted up for our healing and the Banner of our victory. In Him we behold *Yahweh Nissi*—The Lord our *Standard*.

John 12:32–33

And I (Jesus), if I be lifted up from the earth, will draw all men unto Me. This He said, signifying what death He should die (on the rugged wooden Cross).

Galatians 3:13

Christ hath redeemed us from the curse of the law, **being made a curse for us**: for it is written, Cursed is every one that hangeth on a tree:

We can't deny that we too have been poisoned by snakes—the snakes of strict religious liturgy and churchianity. We have been poisoned by our binding traditions and programs that only exist to please us. But the Spirit is telling us now to look up to that ridiculed, *cursed posture of worship* that many refuse to identify themselves with. Why? because they consider it shameful, even disgraceful, to be undone before the Lord. Clearly, they do not know the heart and mind of the Holy Spirit. They do not see that this very posture is *the Degel and the Nûs of God that ushers in the Glory*. Not many want to behold the *serpent on the pole—the worship posture*. It is treated as accursed and forbidden. And yet, tragically, many would rather embrace the *poison of religion and denominational protocol* than receive the *redemption of Revival*.

May I speak freely? Leaders who lack the revelation of this holy posture will inevitably struggle to discover its true Power. And as a result, a true worshipper may find themselves being stared at with contempt and displeasure (Isaiah 29:13–14). My prayer is that such leaders will come to understand the significance of *the posture that attracts, hosts and releases the Glory*.

Think of how the Colours of a regiment are honoured. They made the soldier stand up tall with confidence, his posture in tune with the spirit and ethos of the regiment. He knew in his heart that he was a part of something special and unique. This authentic place set him apart from those not in the regiment. He belonged to something of great value. Even if he did not fully grasp its power, he felt the strength of the banner and honoured it with the dignity it deserved. His life was given to his regiment; he was willing to lay it down for the regiment's cause. And the flag would remain the representative symbol of him, of every soldier that came before him, and all of those who would come after him.

Just as the Royal Ensign embodied the life, loyalty, passion, posture, and discipline of the soldier, so too does our worship posture reveal the Glory Carrier—standing strong in God's Army of Glory Carriers, commissioned to carry and release the Glory into the nations.

In the same way, *we must honour our place of Power with God—that holy worship posture*. It must be held as sacred and venerated as holy before the Lord, for it is none other than the *Standard—the Degel and Nûs* of God.

> **REVIVAL TRUTH:**
>
> " The Glory *recognises the posture*. The Glory *responds to* the posture and the Glory *communes with* our worship posture.

Yahweh Nissi, is asking, "Who will ascend to the Hill of the Lord? Who will adopt the Revival posture?" The answer is clear: the worship posture is *the Revival Posture*. But be warned—you will be mocked and called accursed, like that cursed serpent on the *pole* (*Nês*). You may be labelled as strange, unprincipled, or aberrant—but are you willing to lay down your life as *God's pioneer-leaders and worship warriors,* unafraid to demonstrate the posture that hosts the Glory?

Our worship posture is *God's Revival Ensign* to the nations. If you are willing to accept it, the Spirit has already proclaimed this Truth to you. Let him who has ears hear what the Spirit is saying to the Churches (Matthew 11:14–15).

Arise! Take your place on the Hill of the Lord. Be God's Banner of Revival! Let your worship posture release the Fire of God's Glory into the nations—undaunted and unashamed! The Glory is ready, and He will be revealed through you!

PART 9   *The Posture that Attracts, Hosts, & Releases the Glory*

Prayer:
Jesus, we humble our hearts before You. We understand that our worship posture is Your Standard (*the Degel and Nûs*) for Revival. Jesus be glorified in our worship... Amen.

May the Lord Lift Up His Standard Through You. For the Great Day of His Visitation Draws Near!

The Spirit of the Lord Shall Raise A Standard   CHAPTER 19

'The Glory of the Uncut Stone, where the Lord has recorded His Name'

CHAPTER 20

The Uncut Stone

The Spirit of Prophecy (and the Mantle of the Revivalist) will be the shaking of the leaders of the Churches.

When God was instructing Moses on how to build His Altar, the Lord wanted it to be *authentic:* He required that it be made of *Uncut Stone—natural and untouched by man's tools.* (Note the bolded)

Exodus 20:24–25

An Altar of earth thou shalt make unto Me, and shalt sacrifice thereon thy burnt offerings, and thy peace offerings, thy sheep, and thine oxen: **in all places where I record My Name I will come unto thee, and I will bless thee.** And if thou wilt make Me an Altar of stone, **thou shalt not build it of hewn stone: for if thou lift up thy tool upon it, thou hast polluted it**.

The uncut stone represents an *unrestricted worshipper*—one who worships God with all of their heart, mind and soul (John 4:23–24). Authentic, unrestricted worship is the posture that truly *hosts the Glory of God*. It does not depend on programs, polished presentations, or favoured speakers. It depends only on the leading of the Spirit. For where the Spirit leads, there the Spirit moves (2 Corinthians 4:5–6).

By contrast, the cut stone reflects man's preference: a reliance on structure, program, and control. Program-driven ministers may prefer a service that is neat and predictable, rather than a Holy-Spirit-shaking service. I know that you're praying for Revival, but a program-driven mindset cannot accommodate, nor can it birth, a Move of God. Only *the Worship Posture* that hosts the Presence can do this. If you prioritise duty-to-program over encounter, you will forever be praying for Revival and yet never experience it. Programs can't impart Revival Knowledge; only His Presence does.

Desperation for Revival is often the clearest sign that Revival is near. Perhaps that is exactly what you need—a hunger in your soul so deep that you refuse to settle for man-centred, culture-driven worship. Instead, let that holy desperation drive you back to your true posture of worship. And when you do, the Revival Fire will flow to you like rivers, because God always responds to authentic worship.

> "God always responds to authentic worship.

The Holy One is looking from Heaven and asking, "Where is the place of My Rest? Where is the heart that trembles at My Word? Where is My Altar, which is made of uncut stones? For I desire to record My Name there, and make Myself known to My people" (Isaiah 66:1–2).

Leaders of the Church—you have followed your programs and traditions, and you have entertained the masses, yet no Fire has fallen. Now, a *prophetic confrontation* has come to you, like Mount Carmel, and the Holy Spirit is speaking plainly: "How long will you waver between two opinions? If the Lord is God, follow Him. But if your way is preferred, then follow it." (1 Kings 18:21). The Fire is ready to fall—it is time to draw near, lay aside your man-made altar, and choose Him (1 Kings 18:28–38).

> **REVIVAL TRUTH:**
>
> "If you prioritise duty-to-program over Encounter, you will forever be praying for Revival and see no result.

I marvel at how rigid many of you have become—rigid in the sense that your polished programs lack the discernment of the Spirit's Presence. Oh, fathers of the House… It seems the very thing you *mastered* has now mastered you. The very system you harnessed with perfection has put a bridle on you. This causes me to wonder: "What form of Revival are you really praying for, that is supposed to agree with your form of worship?"

I speak to you with all my heart, for Authentic Worship is about to break upon the Body of Christ and set many free. Fresh Oil from the Holy Ghost is ready to pour upon many. "Behold, I will do a new thing: now it shall spring forth; shall ye not know it?" (Isaiah 43:18-19). And the Spirit of God is waiting for you to discern this critical hour—this season of seasons that has come to us. Oh, that you would not let Him just pass you by without reaching for the edge of His garment. Oh, that you would lay hold of Him in this great hour of turning.

PART 9   *The Posture that Attracts, Hosts, & Releases the Glory*

God Wants A Pure Offering

Malachi 1:10 (English Standard Version)

Oh, that there were one among you who would shut the [Temple] doors, that you might not kindle fire on My Altar *in vain!* I have no pleasure in you, says the LORD of hosts, and I will not accept an offering from your hand.

In the days of the prophet Malachi, the priests no longer carried out their duties with sincerity of heart. To them, it was all superficial—surface worship. They conducted their priestly duties hastily, without interest or depth of heart. They were simply going through the motions and religiously ticking boxes on a to-do list. A crippling complacency had settled in.

As a result, *the dynamic, pioneering spirit* of authentic worship became blunt, growing dull, out of touch, distant and deteriorated. The most glorious ministry—the worship of God—was no longer in the heart of man. That's what happens when what is meant to move the heart becomes disengaged and distant from its original purpose: it loses its true meaning.

The priests had polluted the offering by treating lightly the very thing meant to hold the highest place before God—*worship from the heart*. They thought it insignificant to present sick, blind and lame animals to the Lord. Their hearts had grown cold and uncaring. Passion, honour, hunger, and reverence toward God had vanished, replaced only by a sense of religious duty to be fulfilled (Malachi 1:6-9). But the Lord looked upon them with great disappointment and intense displeasure. He desired a pure offering. And if the priests of Israel weren't going to do it correctly, God would gladly receive this pure offering from the Gentiles.

Malachi 1:11 (KJV)

From the rising of the sun even unto the going down of the same, My Name shall be great among the Gentiles; and in every place incense shall be offered unto My Name, and *a pure offering:* for My Name shall be great among the heathen, saith the LORD of hosts.

This is not something to dismiss lightly. If God wanted the Temple Doors shut because of polluted worship, then these Words carry a profound message for us today.

"Worship has a high place in God.

Consider how serious God's Words were toward the priests in dealing with their waywardness, "Shut the doors [of the Temple]... I have no pleasure in you...I will not accept your offering." The Lord was calling for a shutdown of every form of worship that did not please Him. And He is doing the same today. He will not accept a polluted offering. Given the seriousness of this matter, we must, with the fear of God and with due diligence, repair and restore the Altar of our heart's posture, and offer unto the Lord the pure offering of our surrendered hearts!

If the Lord Jesus didn't hesitate to openly rebuke the Seven Churches, I am certain He will not hesitate to rebuke you as well (Revelation 2–3). The Holy Spirit may speak plainly and say to you without hesitation, "You have become blind and unable to see" (Isaiah 6:9). "You blind guides! Which is greater, your traditions of conformity, or the *Altar of a heart* that hosts the Glory? Yet, the Truth remains firm—*it is the Altar of the heart that sanctifies the gift*" (Matthew 23:19–20).

PART 9　　*The Posture that Attracts, Hosts, & Releases the Glory*

"The condition to receive Revival is to have a tender heart before God. It is this tenderness that allows you to recognise the Glory in your midst.

Spiritual hunger is the willingness to receive...the Spirit works there. I plead with you: do not settle. The boldness and Power of the Spirit of the Lord Jesus is passing by right before you. Will you reach out like Bartimaeus? *He recognised the Anointing of the Revivalist*—Jesus Christ. He did not dismiss Jesus as merely another man from Nazareth. When Jesus walked through Jericho, many would have asked, "What good thing can come out of Nazareth?" But Bartimaeus knew better. He was tired of his blindness and *longed to see*. Perhaps he sensed a gentle prompting from the Holy Spirit.

As soon as he realised it was Jesus, he refused to let his limitations hinder his expectation. Bartimaeus honoured *the Messiah* by seizing *the Revelation of Revival* before him. He cried out with great expectation, *"Yeshua! Son of David,* have mercy on me!" This is the attitude the Lord expects from us if we are to receive the Revival Fire. Bartimaeus could not afford to be cautious or conservative—he needed to act immediately. There and then, the transformation began when he called out to the Lord with all his heart (Mark 10:46–52).

Saints, perhaps you have already called out to the Holy Spirit and are now postured to receive Him. The Spirit has turned toward you and is standing before you, saying, "Here I am. What can I do for you?"

> **REVIVAL TRUTH:**
>
> "Only one thing attracts the Glory of God: a broken and humble posture before the Living God.

He Knows Our Hearts

> **REVIVAL TRUTH:**
> "God is not drawn by the loudness of our voices or by the eloquence of our words, but by the posture of our hearts

We can speak truth, but our motives never lie. We can be gentle as doves, but our motives never lie. We can quote every Revival scripture, but our motives never lie. We can preach love and unity, honour and empathy, but our motives never lie. We can call on the name of Jesus and desire healing, but our motives never lie. We can groan for Revival from dusk till dawn, but our motives never lie. We can claim that we pursue Revival, but our motives never lie.

The Lord will be real, raw, and authentic with you. His Fire is not a gimmick for attraction—*He must cleanse us to empower us.*

The Holy Spirit knows our hearts. He knows our true posture before Him. Nothing is hidden. Every work, every word, every intention is manifest before His Presence. The Fire of God does not respond to many words—it only responds to an authentic heart that speaks the language and heartbeat of the Spirit of God. There is only one thing that attracts the Glory of God: a broken and humble posture before the Living God—that's pure offering. For the Glory shall come and abide upon those who have *learnt how to behold the Abiding Word.*

Friends, we must not make the mistake of straying from His *Abiding Presence*. If we must preach, let our message be about our posture before Him, for it is the Lord alone who can pour upon us the riches of His Glory and Grace.

Standing on the summit of this great *Prophetic Call and Mandate*, I cannot hold back from testifying of the Fire of God. It's time to respond to the Lord's *invitation* to ascend to the Hill of His Glory. I can't think of anything more glorious than to be *baptised* with the Commissioning Fire of His Holy Presence (Exodus 3, Acts 2). Oh, what joy it is to know that the Lord Himself will draw near to us again. And when He comes, may He find us in a *broken and humble posture* (James 4:8, Isaiah 66:1–2). For I am convinced that God is not drawn by the loudness of our voices or the eloquence of our words, but by the posture of our hearts (1 Corinthians 2:1–5).

Glory! Glory! Glory! The awe-inspiring and magnificent *Day of the Great Awakening* is at hand. Let our hearts rise to meet the King of Glory, for the time of fulfilment draws near, and the *Dawn of the New Day* is ready to burst forth upon the Earth. May the Lord turn hearts to make many ready to receive the fullness of *His Great Revival Fire* (Ephesians 3:17–19). Let Heaven and Earth resound with praise—**Hallelujah! Amen!**

May You Be A Pure And Pleasing Offering to the Lord, the King of Glory.

The Uncut Stone   CHAPTER 20

Part 10 – The Credo & Passion of the Revivalist

"Oh, that I may burn with the Fires of the Burning Bush— that same Glorious Fire of the Upper Room. Jesus... All I want is to behold the Glory of Your Word in the midst of Your people."

CHAPTER 21

The Praying Preacher

May you be clothed with the Power that resides
at the Fireplace of your prayerfulness.

Revival comes from the *birth pangs of the Presence-pursuing —Praying Preacher*. This is the preacher who has sought to see the Face of God like Moses did, because a deep longing for God has gripped him.

I pray for you, my fellow brethren in the Lord, that you will have this same pressing desire and posture before the Lord. I pray that your heart be softened to hear His Voice in this critical hour. My unceasing prayers are also for those who have yet to say "Yes" to Jesus through the preaching and testimony of the dedicated *Praying Preacher*. May you be God's messenger of good tidings, ordained by the Lord to bring a true Word burning from *the Fireplace* of His Presence. May you preach only what the Lord wants.

In truth, we should never have to strive for words, for the Spirit already knows what He wants to say. And the Holy Ghost doesn't want you to trouble yourself with earthly words, striving at the pulpit. For *powerful preaching* at the pulpit is meant to be a representation of the *Fireplace of the prayerfulness of the preacher*. He wants you to preach a Word *in season, filled with the Fire of God*. You can only do this by discerning the Word present in the room and burning in you.

Yet, many preachers have dissociated themselves from this wonderful place—the Power of the Word. They have cut themselves off from the life-giving flow of the Holy Spirit. When they preach, they want it to be with great fluency and depth. But it is only *surface-level* revelation, lacking the true depth and substance of the Holy Spirit (1 Corinthians 2:1–5).

The reason is that many preachers have forgotten and abandoned *the Altar of prayerfulness, which is the Fireplace of His Presence*. How is it that we have loved the commendations of the pulpit—the sweet acknowledgements from man—more than the *communion of the Fireplace* of the prayer closet? Yet a life lived in the Spirit of the Word will always be nourished by the Holy Spirit, even amid the persecutions pressing against it.

Truthfully, I have observed that many have forgotten the Power of the prayer closet. We have pursued the ambition to gain notability but forgotten *the art of the prayerful warrior.* Don't be mistaken: no matter how well prepared a sermon is, eloquence cannot replace *the Fire* of the praying preacher. A preacher drenched with the Fire of the Anointing is one who has been soaked in the flames of his prayer life.

> **REVIVAL TRUTH:**
>
> " A preacher drenching with the Fire of the Anointing, is a preacher who has been soaked in the flames of his prayer life.

Prayerfulness prepares the way for *the Waves*. And the Waves of His Presence will not come until and unless we become those given to entering into the Fires of the Most High. We must have the desire to go deeper into the Waters of His Presence (Ezekiel 47).

We may be alone when we preach, but we are not alone when we pray. A preacher who feels lonely without the Anointing is a preacher who has become like the prodigal son. He has forgotten the beautiful vineyards of his prayer life. He has forgotten the courts of his Father's House, where the Voice of Counsel flows unto the Table of Abundance. For where there is counsel, there is abundance. And is not the Holy Spirit our Comforter and Counsellor, waiting for the prodigals to return? Even the preachers have become prodigals because we have loved the loud praises of man more than the inner working of the Spirit's conviction.

The prayerless preacher preaches to impress; the prayerful preacher preaches to *impact*. And let's be clear: this powerlessness at the pulpit is lukewarmness. It has been the contaminated workings of a *prayerless* man, who seeks to incite a pursuit for God but lacks the disciplines of the Fireplace of prayerfulness.

We have strayed away from *the Diamond* of the Spirit, which cannot be attained through fleshly, intellectual efforts. For where the weakness of God is, man's strength barely reaches (Isaiah 55:8–9, 1 Corinthians 1:25). Have we forgotten that man by his own efforts cannot reach the great waterfalls of God's Presence unless he embarks on a Spirit-authored and Spirit-ordained mission to find God (Jeremiah 29:12–13)? Assuredly, this holy place is found in brokenness before the Presence of the all-knowing and all-powerful God.

Jude 1:20

But ye, beloved, building up yourselves on your most holy faith, praying in the Holy Ghost,

In your praying, you may wrestle with God, but be assured you will come forth to the pulpit with Strength and Fire from the Holy Ghost. *Wrestle with God,* oh preacher! *Wrestle until God speaks.*

Don't shake hands with complacency, nor settle with the bread of lukewarmness, for complacency is the fruit of prayerlessness. Don't settle for stale meat and bread. As God's minister, you are supposed to bring fresh bread and meat for the people. Are we not afraid of God? Isn't the House of God the House of fresh Bread—*Bethlehem? The Anointing (the Word-Carrying Mantle)* must be born in the *Manger of our Fireplace*— from a humble, yet *ordained* Bethlehem.

Incline your ears, oh Saints of God... The Fireplace of your prayerfulness carries Holy Ghost influence and impact. Revival Fire remains unquenched and blazing at the Fireplace of prayerfulness. It is your *Secret Place* with God. Although no eyes see, no ears hear, and none perceives the burden which you carry in secret, still, there is One who is attentive to your words. Be still, oh faithful praying preacher...The Glory of God is there to meet you in that place of steadfastness (Matthew 6:6). That precious place of your brokenness is the most beautiful, captivating place in God's eyes. That sacred posture of worship will pour forth pure Anointing Oil and refreshing Words flowing like rivers. Then you will be able to say, "The *Gushing* of the Lord is great upon my being, and His Fire burns fiercely in my bones. My cup overflows."

> **REVIVAL TRUTH:**
> " Prayerfulness is intimacy with God.

In your worship posture, you may be bent under a burden from the Spirit, your flesh dealt a mighty blow *of rebuke and conviction,* but the cleansing will bring forth an unquenchable Fire of the Holy Ghost—a Fire that must burn, and burn bright for many to see.

Hallelujah! Let the scales of delusion and religion fall before a praying preacher consumed with the Fire of God, drenched with abundant Grace, and transformed by Spirit-life. Indeed, consciousness of the nearness of God is wisdom to those who have made His Presence their home. We cannot deny this truth: without the Fires of our prayerfulness, there is no Fire to preach. A house *of Fire* is a house *on fire*. You cannot get a fiery preacher unless you deep him into a fiery furnace of prayer, Word and worship—these three elements are found in the prayer closet.

And just like the great Altar of Mount Carmel, which was first drenched in water, ready to receive the baptism of the Fire, let our lives also be baptised into *the Unction* of His Power through our unceasing prayerfulness. Oh, preacher…you can't be on fire without the Fire of God unless you first be drenched in *the Waters of His Deep Counsels*—the Altar of Mount Carmel must be drenched with *Water* to receive the *Fire*. It would be naive to think otherwise that the Fire is not necessary. But there is no substitute that can measure up to the Fire of God—none comes close.

> **REVIVAL TRUTH:**
> " Without the Fires of our prayerfulness, there is no Fire to preach.

Deepening that thought: where there is restriction in the spirit realm, it is because of a lack of prayerfulness—and the reverse is also true. An unceasing burden for breakthrough must grip our very being. It is the kind of burden that causes us to yield to the Holy Ghost and persist in prayer until a breakthrough comes. That, my friends, is the attitude of the praying preacher. For where there are no flames of prayer, there is no breakthrough to look forward to.

The evangelist Leonard Ravenhill said it this way, "The tragedy of this late hour is that we have too many *dead* men in the pulpits giving too many *dead* sermons to too many *dead* people... *Preacher, with all thy getting—get Unction...(And) Unction cannot be learned, only earned—by prayer.*"[13]

Our prayer and worship life is the junction: the meeting place of the Spirit and us.

> **"**Out from *the junction* of our 'meeting place' with God flows *the Unction* of the Holy Ghost.

There, we receive the Divine not only as a message, but *with Fire*—ignited in us to burn. When we are ignited by the blessed Fire of the Spirit, we become like the prophet Jeremiah, whose very bones were thoroughly soaked with the Fire of the Word. Jeremiah was gloriously helpless—in the best way—when he declared: "Your Word, Lord, was like Fire in my bones; I could not hold it back any longer (Jeremiah 20:9)."

Arise, praying preacher! For Mount Carmel was an Altar prepared with prayerfulness. The Upper Room, too, was an Altar prepared with prayer. And where there is prayerfulness, there is *an open portal*—the door by which the King of Glory enters to minister His Living Word (Psalms 24:7–10). When He ministers, it will be Words of Life and Power—bringing healing and deliverance. They are Words that set the captives free and bind up the brokenhearted. Holy Words poured out like Anointing Oil upon those who mourn with great sorrow. For the Spirit of the Lord desires to clothe them with a garment of comfort for their grief (Isaiah 61:1–3).

Oh, that you would realise, that *the prayer-closet is Home for the Christian*. And if you have wandered like a prodigal son, may the *Fires of Home* call you back. Return, oh one who loves the Presence of the Divine. Return to *your place of Origin in the Holy Ghost*. For in that place, our identity is unquestionable, and our quest to achieve great things, undisputed. There in that humble and holy place, our worship meets the King of Glory. Return, oh lover of God's heart. Come to the Fair One, the Great I Am and be clothed with His garments of praise, and washed with His Words of Life gushing forth from His Presence. Let your prayerfulness meet the Divine. Hold in highest esteem Heaven's most favourable place for you. Let go of your ashes and receive beauty from His gracious and loving Hands. Remove the shoes of your natural thinking and enter boldly into *Holy Grounds* where the Revival Fire is ready to commune with you.

Let my words be more than a sentiment and more than a passionate plea. Be not silent before God, oh praying preacher. *Wrestle with Him*, oh Fire Carrier! *Wrestle till God speaks!* For when He speaks, it becomes a defining moment. It is *defining*, because His Word burns like Fire on the inside of us. This is what the Fireplace of prayerfulness produces. There, in holy and cherished moments, the Spirit nourishes us with the goodness of His Glory. I desire this for you, oh beloved saints of God. For the Fire of the Burning Bush is ordained for you also.

I too have marvelled at the story of the Burning Bush, which was *burning* but not burnt. And the same Fire must come upon us to burn us, not to be burnt but *to remain burning*. For what must be burnt up are the works of the flesh; and what must remain is pure worship unto God.

The Upper Room Fire

The Upper Room also was God's Burning Bush. There, He set ablaze one hundred twenty saints who *beheld* and *received* the fullness of His enduing Power. Those who approached to see what was happening eventually came under the influence of that *Burning Fire*—for they too burned with conviction flowing from that Abiding Fire resting upon them.

> **"**It's one thing to behold the Fire from a distance. It's another thing to approach the Fire and be invited to enter into a conversation with the Glory of God.

The Burning Bush was necessary, and so was the Upper Room. The Fire that the saints met with, was *the commissioning Fire that sent them*. It was a soul-winning, soul-saving Fire resting upon them. A shaking like no other was experienced when the Fire rested upon them. That Holy Fire from Heaven cleansed hearts as the Word went forth. It transformed lives as it broke through the thickness of religion and idolatry. A true Fire, like Mount Carmel, had come in the midst of God's people. It shook nations as steadfast *praying preachers* carried the Flame. They may have come face to face with strong forces of darkness, but God's *Fiery Ones* were not afraid to do mighty exploits for their Saviour. They too were soaked with Power, for *the Spirit's Words were like Fire in their bones*, and they too could not restrain nor withhold the flowing Fire of God.

> **REVIVAL TRUTH:**
>
> **"Souls don't respond to the Altar Call, they respond to the Fire coming from the Altar.**

So, if you reject the posture and life of a praying preacher, you are rejecting the Fire that comes from prayerfulness. And if you refuse the ethos and disciplines of prayerfulness, you will become a place *without Fire*. Be aware also: where there is no Fire, there is no incense ascending to the Throne of God. But for those who honour the sweet fragrance of the Spirit, know very well that it flows from their prayerfulness. (Note the bolded words)."

Revelation 8:3–5

And another angel came and stood at the Altar, having a golden censer; and there was given unto him much incense, that **he should offer it with the prayers of all saints upon the golden Altar which was before the Throne. And the smoke of the incense, which came with the prayers of the saints, ascended up before God** out of the angel's hand. And the angel took the censer, and filled it with fire of the altar, and cast it into the earth: and there were voices, and thunderings, and lightnings, and an earthquake.

As our prayers ascend like incense unto the Lord, our eyes are fixed on Him. For when we *behold Him*, the preaching flows. When we *behold Him*, healing comes…There is Power present when we simply behold His Glory at work in us.

But, I must emphasise: it is an *unhindered and unceasing beholding* of Him. When the praying preacher becomes *aware* of the Fire burning within, he will go forth to the pulpit carrying that glorious Fire, to release it to God's people. His beholding of the Fire releases the powerful force of that Fire. Because *the Fire within* preaches better than the preacher himself. And from that soaking Fire comes the overflow![12]

The Praying Revivalist

*The Revivalist—God's Leader—*is also God's *Praying Preacher and powerful Prayer Warrior.* The Fire he carries will provide its own platform to speak.

"The Fire speaks, and the Fire will prophesy.

> **REVIVAL TRUTH:**
> "The Fire within preaches better than the preacher himself.

The Praying Revivalist follows the model left by his spiritual fathers: **God's leaders are first prayer warriors before they become preaching warriors.** They first learnt how to *move* Heaven with their heart posture and persistent faith. That's when Heaven *moved through them* to bring Revival: breakthrough, healing, deliverance and restoration. Revivalists understand the supreme importance and power of prayer. They know that the effectiveness of their *preaching ministry* flows directly from the effectiveness of their *praying ministry.* They were the leaders of prayer meetings before they became anointed preachers called to go forth and minister God's Word. They were on their faces before the Lord *when the Glory fell,* and commissioned them to go forth and release God's Power.

> May the Powerful Anointing of the Praying Preacher
> Be Yours, And May You Walk In the Glory of His
> Great Awakening Fire!

ENDNOTE:
13.   (Ravenhill, L, 1959, 1987. Chapter One, *Why Revival Tarries,* Bethany House Publishers, 11400 Hampshire Avenue South Bloomington, Minnesota, USA. p.20).

'If you want depth, prepare! If you want depth, take the Fireplace of your prayer closet seriously.'

CHAPTER 22

Preparation & Depth of the Praying Preacher

I have put My Words in your mouth.

It was on a particular Sunday. My family and I had decided to visit another Church in the City. I often get those promptings to go and be with the brethren to support them—no agendas, just pure love for them. I love the unity of the brethren—because I have seen what true unity can accomplish (Psalms 133). *Kingdom unity* shakes cities and transforms lives. You can't have *the blessing of Revival* without true unity. The saints in the Upper Room entered the blessing of this Truth when *their hearts united* to receive the Spirit (Acts 2:1–3).

Back to the story… That Sunday, as my family and I sat among the brethren, a thought from the Spirit began to work in me: "If I gave you all the meetings you wanted to preach in, and you became so busy preaching, I wouldn't be able to produce in you *the fullness* that I desire. But if I keep you hidden for long enough until the time is right, then I will produce in you what I want—it will be filled with My Power. The reason I hid you for a season was to produce *the fruit I wanted."*

This was a phenomenal thought, profoundly spoken into my spirit. Truly, only the Spirit can speak like this. He is purposeful, thoughtful, and deliberate in all that He does.

> "If DEPTH is what God is going to produce in you, it is necessary for Him to hide you for a season.

Now, God spoke to me this way because I hadn't been very active and itinerant with ministry for a season. The reason was simple: God had me on *assignment to write this book, and I knew I could not be released until it was complete.* I sensed that this was His intention and direction, and I was happy to comply and be content.

But I must admit, there were times when I doubted whether the Lord was truly at work. But as I stayed the course. I discovered that Heaven was working so profoundly in the stillness of the wilderness. In that quietness, my heart could hear His Voice speak so powerfully to me.

I reflect on how little I could see when I first entered that quiet place. How my thoughts paled in comparison to His. I saw only what was in front of me, but He saw above and beyond. He had ordained magnificence of me, and was working it out in the crucible of my moulding.

Those quiet moments became powerful encounters— overshadowed by the grandeur of the Spirit's Voice speaking so powerfully into my spirit. In that while I remained hidden, pioneering the unknown in silence, God was doing *a mighty work in me.* I felt that He had chosen to keep me hidden for *His Purpose, and not mine.* They were His thoughts—*Deep Thoughts.*

If *depth* was what He intended to produce in me, then being hidden was necessary. For I felt that even in my hiddenness, His eyes looked gracefully upon my unperfected life. And in His Book, something extraordinary was written of me…for me. "For You have possessed my reins; You have covered me in *the womb of Your Fire.*"

Thus, I will yet praise Him—for I am fearfully and wonderfully made in *the secret place* of His Presence. Indeed, how marvellous are His Works; and that my soul knows right well that His Ways are higher than mine.

Even in this silence, my life was never hidden from Him. I was being transformed from Glory to Glory in secret, in the crucible of His Fire that was calling me deeper. Now I marvel at the wonder of His Glory and Grace working so powerfully in me, curiously wrought in *the Secret Place* of *Abba*, the Most High (Psalms 139:13-16, Psalms 91:1).

In those many hours of quiet and beautiful communion, torrents of His magnificent Power flowed so abundantly through my being. My heart was warmed and greatly encouraged. And I quietly said to the Lord: "If this is the case, then keep me hidden until You are ready… I prefer to be hidden."

> "The man destined for great exploits is the man hidden by God for a season. At the appointed time, he shall be revealed —for great exploits always follow the man of depth.

I pray that this testimony will be imparted to you as *precious deposits* from His Heart to yours. This is rare, profound, and deeply personal. God is wholeheartedly *personal and relational* when He speaks to us. His Personality is woven throughout Scripture, revealing Him as both deeply *personal and abundantly merciful* (Psalms 145:9).

Personal and relational? Yes…When He said,
- "I am with you to always, even unto the end" (Matthew 28:20).
- "Be still and know that I am God" (Psalms 46:10).

- "Fear not, I have redeemed you. I have called you by name, you are Mine" (Isaiah 43:1).
- When you pass through the waters, I will be with you" (Isaiah 43:2).
- "…ask for the ancient paths, where the good way is, and walk in it, and you will find rest for your souls" (Jeremiah 6:16 NIV).
- "… I have loved you with an everlasting love, and with lovingkindness have I drawn you" (Jeremiah 31:3).
- "… I will bless you and make your name great…"(Genesis 12:2).
- "Enlarge the place of your tent" (Isaiah 54:2).
- "My Presence shall go with you, and I will give you rest" (Exodus 33:14).
- "Behold, there is a place by Me, and you shall stand upon a rock…" (Exodus 33:21).

The Lord wants to speak to us in this deeply personal and relational way, just as He did with Adam in the beginning. What defined Adam was already known in God; it was a design deeply rooted in *communion, companionship, closeness, and camaraderie with God*.

Everything you need is there—where He is. *Direction* is already before you, for God Himself is direction. So stay *the course*, and *steady the posture of your heart on Him* (Isaiah 26:3). He knows what He is doing in your life and what He desires to produce in you. As you endure, the Spirit is at work cultivating wisdom, resilience and maturity through your patience and your diligence.

Jeremiah 1:8–10

Be not afraid of their faces: for I am with thee to deliver thee, saith the LORD. Then the LORD put forth His Hand and touched my mouth. And the

LORD said unto me, Behold, I have put My Words in thy mouth. See, I have this day set thee over the nations and over the kingdoms, to root out, and to pull down, and to destroy, and to throw down, to build, and to plant.

If You Want Depth—Prepare

Matthew 6:5–6
And when thou prayest, thou shalt not be as the hypocrites are: for they love to pray standing in the synagogues and in the corners of the streets, that they may be seen of men. Verily I say unto you, They have their reward. But thou, when thou prayest, enter into thy closet, and when thou hast shut thy door, pray to thy Father which is in secret; and thy Father which seeth in secret shall reward thee openly.

If you desire to be used mightily by the Lord, make your secret place your *most frequently visited* place. If you want depth, take the Fireplace of your prayer closet seriously. Abide there until the Fire of God consumes you thoroughly. Over the many years that I have walked with the Lord, I have found this to be true: profound Spirit-knowledge and Power rest upon a vessel who has gone through the fire of their moulding—most prominently in the secret place with God. It is a necessary work of the Spirit of God. He wants to raise prayerful preachers carrying *Holy Spirit Depth*.

"If you want depth, *prepare!*

Know that *the Fire* you're carrying is a better preacher than you could ever be. For the Fire of the Holy Ghost is bold and relentless. Hallelujah! The Fire *preaches* and the Fire *prophesies*, the Fire *heals* and the Fire *transforms*.

A *priming* is taking place over nations and cities, and over specific Churches and individuals. A *preparation* like no other has been ongoing in the realm of the spirit. It's a preparation to receive you—the Burning Ones. The fiery Word—shut up in your bones, is being prepared for a people. And at the appointed time of *God's Visitation*, that Word burning in you will be released. (Jeremiah 29:10). Indeed, an intense and immense level of God's Power is ready to be unleashed.

> **REVIVAL TRUTH:**
> " A priming or preparation guided by the Holy Spirit will lead to the fulfilment of the Glory Mandate.

The Hiding Place of His Purpose

"Depth with God is found in the hiding place of His Purpose.

When we become truly hungry for that *Place of Depth in God, true recognition from Heaven finds us.* And while you wait and remain hidden, Power from Heaven descends upon that quiet place to commune with you and to do a mighty work in you. Stay hidden, man of God… Stay hidden, woman of God! For God is about to launch you into greater heights, clothed with the Power of His Revival Anointing.

Psalms 32:7–8

"Thou art my Hiding Place; Thou shalt preserve me from trouble; Thou shalt compass me about with songs of deliverance. Selah. (The Lord says) I will instruct thee and teach thee in the way which thou shalt go: I will guide thee with Mine Eye."

I speak to you, oh powerful preacher of God... Don't you know that ravens (of fresh revelation) have been appointed to bring you special food at the hiding place of your brook (1 Kings 17:2–6)? God has intended *Peculiar revelation* to fill your heart and overflow from you. His breakthrough thoughts have been appointed for you.

So, if your prayer closet is your most cherished place, expect peculiar revelation to flow like rivers. I exhort you to make your prayer closet a high priority and adorn it with the truthfulness of your heart before God.

> **REVIVAL TRUTH:**
>
> " The effectiveness of your preaching ministry comes from the effectiveness of your praying ministry.

Doing Church without revelation is building without the help of the Holy Spirit—it may look good, but it lacks Holy Spirit depth. Don't be fooled: the esteemed oil of human clergy-ness cannot produce Power. Only the *fullness of the Fireplace of God's Presence can nourish and empower.* It is the Holy Ghost, working in a vessel drenched in prayer, who releases genuine Spirit-depth—the kind of depth that transforms lives. And, when you take the things of the Spirit seriously, what overflows from your life impacts every room you walk into. That, my friends, is true profoundness—from Heaven's perspective (John 7:38–39).

This reminds me of the story of the pot of oil that poured supernaturally to fill every vessel in the room (2 Kings 4:1–7). That single pot only began to flow without limits because the *Word of the Spirit* rested on it—and all of this happened behind closed doors. That oil poured unceasingly and increasingly in that secret place, where vessels were *made available to receive it*. This vividly illustrates how the Anointing works also. In the same way, the Anointing intensifying in your life is appointed to bring deliverance and breakthrough to all who will align their hearts with the Revival Mantle. Preachers, let this encourage you: *pursue the hidden life in the Holy Ghost.*

When you do, you won't have to thirst or search anymore because the Fire that communes with you in the secret place will speak powerfully through you. He will move with the might and demonstration of His Glory. For certain that holy Fire will go with you to the pulpit, overflowing with tremendous Heavenly force, ready to fill a room with His Glory. And when you open your mouth to speak, the Fire resting on you will speak (1 Corinthians 2:1–5). This is the splendid work of the Holy Ghost, and it is all for His Glory.

Friends, now is the appointed time! And as you step into this moment, fully clothed with His Fire, remember: **you have been Chosen for such a time as this.**

Get Ready! The Word burning in you is about to transform lives. And when it overflows from you, it shall prosper.

Get Ready! You are going to go forth in joy, and be led forth in peace.

Get Ready! The mountains and hills are about to break forth before you with singing.

Watch and See! The trees of the field are about to clap their hands (Reference Scripture: Isaiah 55:11–13).

Prayer:

Oh, Heavenly Father…stir our hearts to unceasing prayer and may we persist till Your Glory overflows. Cause us to desire after You with all our hearts. For we love Your Presence. Lord, do a deep work in us. We are ready to receive…we are ready.

In Jesus Name, Amen.

May the Powerful Anointing of the Praying Preacher Be Yours, And May You Walk In the Glory of His Great Awakening Fire!

Part 11 – The Word of Glory & The Mantled Vessel

'Behold the Glory of His Word—We have this treasure in earthen vessels.'

CHAPTER 23

Revival Architecture

We have this Treasure in earthen vessels.

For certain, the Lord is calling us back to our original place in Him—to host His Glory once again. And *God wants to speak to us again.* His forthcoming Great Revival is at the *doorstep of our hearts.* He is calling you to lift up your eyes and see. And when you do, you will **behold the Glory of His Word—in the face of Jesus Christ**, *the fullness* of the Glory (John 16:13-15). By fullness, I mean, He is:

- The Kavod (Glory) of the Father,
- The Radiance of the Glory, Who upholds all things by *the Word* of His Power (Hebrews 1:3),
- The King of Glory (The Lord God, Mighty in Battle),
- The Ark of God—the Exemplar of the Glory Carrier.

2 Corinthians 4:6–7

For God, who commanded the Light to shine out of darkness, hath shined in our hearts, to give the Light of the Knowledge of the Glory of God in the Face of Jesus Christ. But **we have this treasure in earthen vessels,** that the excellency of the Power may be of God, and not of us.

The Knowledge of the Glory of Jesus is that treasure carried in our earthen vessels. This is that same Knowledge of the Glory that shall fill the Earth as the waters cover the sea (Habakkuk 2:14). This prophetic Word is the Mandate resting upon us, and is the primary objective of the five-fold ministries (Ephesians 4:11–13).

Notice that there are two distinct components: first, the Church reaching the full stature of the fullness of Christ; second, the Glory filling the Earth. Both are actually within the same complementary mission—to fulfil one is to fulfil the other. In other words, as we reach the fullness of Christ, we simultaneously release the fullness of Christ to the nations.

This allows us to understand fully the grand finale of God's purpose: the Glory shall fully be formed in us and shall fully radiate its brightness through us.

> **"**We are Glory Carriers for a reason—it's about Jesus filling the Earth with His Glory. That is the ultimate goal and the main reason why He gave us Mantles.

I truly desire that this be inscribed upon your hearts by the conviction of the Holy Spirit. The Revival Trumpet is already sounding. Let its powerful *call* reach your heart with *understanding* —the lack of it is the reason why many Churches have not yet seen or experienced Revival. This is why the Holy Spirit needs you to make room for the KNOWLEDGE (revelation) that hosts the GLORY (the Lord's Burden).

The Burden of the Word of Glory

There are three main types of *Prophetic Burdens* that the Lord gives to man:
- **Intercessory Burden**—to pray till breakthrough comes,
- **Prophetic Word**—remains till the Word comes to pass,
- **The Lord's Burden for Revival (The Burden of the Word of Glory)**—conceived in the Revivalist and remains until its fulfilment. It is given specifically to accomplish Revival Assignments (I shared this in Chapter 6, *The Birth of the Move*).

Each of these operates under the same Divine principle declared in Isaiah 55:10–11:

> "…My Word that goes forth out of My Mouth: It shall not return unto Me void, but **It shall accomplish that which I please, and It shall prosper in the thing whereto I sent it.**"

Given this foundational Truth, our focus is on **the Burden of the Word of Glory.** For those seeking Revival, this is *the Word* you must give full attention to. This is no ordinary word. Described more accurately as—the Word of Glory (or, the Lord's Burden) resting upon the Revivalist.

This Word is not the same as Revelational Knowledge. Both are received and proclaimed prophetically. Though both are important and have similarities, they have distinct purposes:
- **The BURDEN of the Word of Glory is for Revival Assignment** and is only given to those carrying *a Revival Mantle*. This is the Glory that comes to rest on the Revivalist's Mantle and becomes *the weighty Word* resting upon his being.

- **REVELATION**, on the other hand, is to impart to us the Knowledge of God, concerning His Glory, and to reveal His Heart and Mind toward us.

Together, these two special attributes of *the Word of Glory* are themed as God's *Axiom—His established decree* for the Revival Mandate.

Habakkuk 2:14
For the Earth shall be filled with the KNOWLEDGE of the GLORY of the Lord, as the waters cover the sea.

In essence, *the knowledge of Revival* imparted to us, prepares our hearts and minds *to receive the Burden of the Lord*—which is **the Glory in the form of a WORD**, deposited into us and intended to be released through us. A metaphor that we can use to illustrate this is *the manger of Christ in Bethlehem, prepared as a resting place to receive Jesus*. In the same way, revelation knowledge is like the manger: ready to receive *the Word made flesh*—the Burden of the Word (Isaiah 66:1-2).

The Isaiah 9:6 prophecy *(which refers to Jesus)*, descriptively captures the manger metaphor, and unveils a beautiful truth about **the Revivalist carrying the Burden of the Word of Glory.** Allow me to share my prophetic interpretation:

> "For unto us 'A BURDEN OF THE WORD OF GLORY' is born, unto us AN APPOINTED REVIVALIST is given: and Christ's Authority shall be placed *as a burden* upon the Revivalist. For Jesus —the Wonderful, Counsellor, the mighty God, the everlasting Father and the Prince of Peace, shall work mightily through His Glory Carriers, to

establish His Kingdom of Peace and Power, with Judgement and Justice forevermore. The Zeal of the Lord of hosts will perform this (through His Holy Spirit working in us)."

A relevant note:
In a similar way that the writer of Hebrew received deeper insight into Psalms 8:4-6 (about a man). The writer beautifully expanded it to reveal that the "man" is Jesus Christ (in Hebrews 2:5-13). Likewise, my inspired interpretation applies prophetic insight. It unveils how God raises and equips His appointed Revivalists to carry His Glory in our generation.

The Highest Point of Our Thinking for Revival

There are four forerunner elements that form the sacred *Revival Architecture*, and must become *the highest point* of our thinking for Revival—without them, there can be no Move of God:
- The Revival Mantle (Anointing) and Mandate.
- The Vessels, marked with the Revival Fire.
- The heart posture that receives, hosts, carries, and releases the Glory.
- God then sends the Burden of the Word of Glory, conceived in the Revivalist in the form of a Power-Carrying Word, to be birthed at the appointed place and time.

"There must be a Revival Mantle (Anointing) placed upon a chosen vessel. This vessel must have the correct heart attitude to host the Burden of the Word of Glory. This kind of Word from God only comes to this kind of Vessel chosen by God.

This is *Divine Order and Divine Protocol*. Revival will not come any other way but through this established *Heavenly Framework*. When all the elements listed above are combined, the result is REVIVAL.

I pray that as you meditate deeply on this, your heart will be stirred to say to the Lord: "Here I am Lord. Use me for Your Glory. Here I am, Lord—send me. I want to be Your Fire Carrier."

Praying What God Wants

Your prayers for Revival should focus on **the Revival Architecture** that I have outlined. You've been praying for Revival, and I acknowledge your unceasing efforts, but now with this added knowledge, you will be *praying correctly* and right on point—what God wants.

Jesus was actually saying it, though I don't think we really understood the key words that need emphasising here,

Luke 10:2
...pray ye therefore the Lord of the harvest, that He would **send forth labourers** into His harvest.

We must pray for the Revivalist...not just for the Revival. We must ask God to send His Fire-Carrying Messenger. It's time to pray with precision, to engage with God correctly on the matter. This is *the knowledge* that God requires us to grasp.

Isaiah 52:6–10 aligns with Jesus's statement in Luke10:2. While the passage is a Messianic prophecy pointing to *Jesus*, it also applies to *the Revivalist*. Allow me to unpack it, bit by bit, to understand its full significance.

Isaiah 52:6–10

Verse 6:
"Therefore My people shall know My Name: therefore they shall know in that Day that *I am He that doth Speak*: behold, it is I."

My insight on verse 6:
[GOD WILL SPEAK. His BURDEN of the Word of Glory shall be sent. And Revival shall come to the People at an appointed time… But how, or through whom shall it come?]

Verse 7:
"How beautiful upon the mountains are *the feet of him* that bringeth good tidings, that publisheth peace; that bringeth good tidings of good, that publisheth salvation; that saith unto Zion, Thy God reigneth!"

My insight on verse 7:
[Revival shall come through the appointed Messenger mantled with The Revival Mandate, carrying good tidings— that specific Burden of the Word of Glory]

Verse 8–9:
"Thy watchmen shall lift up the voice; with the voice together shall they sing: for they shall see eye to eye, when the LORD shall bring again Zion. Break forth into joy, sing together, ye waste places of Jerusalem: for the LORD hath comforted His people, He hath redeemed Jerusalem."

My insight on verses 8–9:
[The watchmen—refers to the ministers and Christians who have been unwavering in their hearts for Revival and have prayed and waited unceasingly for the Revival Fire]

Verse 10:
"The LORD hath made bare His holy Arm in the eyes of all the nations; and all the ends of the Earth shall see the Salvation of our God."

My insight on verse 10:
[God's Holy Arm is the Word of Glory revealed through the Revivalist. When Revival has finally come, then shall God's magnificent Glory be manifested to all nations.]

Now that you understand this, I submit to you that *the Revival Fire* you are seeking is THE BURDEN OF WORD OF GLORY, which must find a *Glory-Carrying Mantle* to rest upon. **This Word must be made flesh, to be received and released.**

This glorious treasure is manifested:
- To reveal and glorify Jesus,
- To fill us (His latter House) with His Glory,
- To make us Glory-Carrying Witnesses for Him,
- For the shaking of the nations, and
- To prepare the Church for Christ's return.

Glory to God in the highest, and on Earth, peace and goodwill to mankind! For the Lord has prepared *Revival Leaders* for the people —He has ordained this *Blessing* to come to you.

Now is the time to respond to the High Call of God. For we all have been summoned by the Holy Ghost to meet Him at the Place Where He has chosen to speak with us. If we are to receive the BLESSING OF HIS GLORY, we must let go of every earthly protocol that falls short of the REVIVAL ARCHITECTURE He has given to us.

What we are addressing here is *a matter of the heart.* Just like what the Lord did at Mount Carmel, where a *prophetic confrontation met the heart of man.* All that happened because the Fire of God fell upon *a prepared Altar* and burned so wonderfully before the people. There, in that holy place, *hearts were turned to behold His Glory, and to worship His magnificence.*

The coming Great Awakening will do the same thing—it will cause a great turning of hearts. This must happen—and it will, through the Burning Ones. They will be like their Lord Jesus, relentlessly compelled to accomplish the purpose of *the Divine Endowment* resting upon them as *favour from Heaven.*

Prayer:

Holy Spirit, I am sorry for limiting you Lord. I am sorry for standing in the way of Your Move. I get myself out of the way, so You can do as You please. Lord I give You my heart. I give myself to you to be fully used for Your Glory, In Jesus Name…Amen.

May the Blessing of His Glory Be Yours!

Part 12 – The Trumpet Sounds – It's Time for Revival!

'Behold, the Lord of Glory will speak again through His Burning Ones.'

CHAPTER 24

The Trumpet Sounds— It's Time for Revival!

It's time for the Lord to SPEAK again.

*I*t's time for the Lord to SPEAK again. Like at Mount Carmel, the shaking of the nations will come through another *prophetic confrontation*. This time, its impact will be unprecedented. And when He speaks, He will speak through His mantled vessels—His Burning Ones.

"The Glory that is coming, has already arrived in those who are now postured to release it as God's prophetic confrontation to the Church—It will be the shaking of the very foundations and framework of the Church.

The prophet Zechariah wrote, "Who hath despised the Day of small things? for they shall rejoice and see the *Plum Line..."That Plum line is the Revivalist Carrying a Mighty Mantle from the Lord, sent to accomplish what God wants* (Zechariah 4:9-10). Indeed, it will surely be a Day of days when a *great igniting of hearts* shall come upon the leaders of the Church. Saints, the great turning of hearts has already started to happen because the Glory is gradually settling on Glory Carriers. *Without the Glory, there will be no turning of hearts.*

And when the appointed time comes for the Great Revival Fire to begin, the Lord will send forth His Burning Ones with His Message of Glad Tidings, and the Spirit shall be poured upon the Altar of our hearts. For the Holy Spirit will speak a mighty Revival Word through His Warrior Leader—the Great Revivalist. This is all known in God's Heart, and we do not need to trouble ourselves over this. It will happen according to His perfect timing—**God's got this.** Our task is to simply step aside and let Him do what He wants.

Through His chosen Army of Glory Carriers, *Adonai Tzva'ot (The Lord of Hosts) shall release His Glory upon the nations.* He shall speak His Word of Glory to His Revival Warriors everywhere. A great posturing will take place in all the nations. It shall be glorious beyond comprehension. I can already hear the sound of hearts surrendering.

> "I love You Lord, and I lift my voice,
> to worship You, o my soul, rejoice.
> Take joy my King, in what You hear.
> May it be a sweet, sweet *sound* in Your Ears."[14]

A thoughtful moment:

Oh, how sweet, is *the Sound of Revival*. Oh, how glorious it will be, when the Name of the Lord Jesus shall be exalted in all nations. It shall be *a pure offering* unto the Lord of Glory.

CHAPTER 24

Malachi 1:11

For from the rising of the sun even unto the going down of the same My Name shall be great among the Gentiles; and in *every place* incense shall be offered unto My Name, and a pure offering: for My Name shall be great among the heathen, saith the LORD of hosts.

The Spirit says, "Come...and be not afraid of this prophetic confrontation. Come and be filled with My Glory." For certain, I will rejoice to see *His Glory-Day*. As God's watchman, I have taken my post upon the watchtower to gaze *attentively* at the Word of Glory (Habakkuk 2:1–3). I have learnt from the Holy Ghost and understood His Heart for Revival. I know His Word will not fail—this Truth brings me great comfort.

Saints of God, our prophet-fathers and apostle-fathers longed to see *this Day*. They are also praying for us even now in Heaven. They are that great cloud of witnesses spoken of in Hebrews 12:1–2. High anticipation is also in their hearts as they behold *the unfolding Scroll of the Great Revival Mandate*. They know it is now our turn to receive the Glory. They, too, have waited patiently for this *Holy Moment to come*. They have patiently waited for *the Dawn of His Light to break forth*... Oh, how wonderful shall that **Glory-Day** be, when the King of Glory shall finally rise upon us with healing in His Wings (Isaiah 60:1-2, Malachi 4:2).

Revival Starts When You Let Go

Apostles, Prophets, Pastors, Teachers and Evangelists...Children of the Most High God... Revival will start when you let go. And you need to let go now! Start by repenting before the Lord for not fully understanding His Heart for Revival. I have said all I can say...

Now, as I present to you this wonderful manifesto on the Great Revival Mandate and the Mantle to carry it, I will say it plainly again: **You need your Revival Leaders. You need Fathers of the Move who will mentor you into the Move of God.** Seek the Lord for these individuals. This is about honouring what God honours and pursuing what God wants. With all due respect, this is God's business—it was never ours in the first place. It started in Him, and it will end in Him: the Alpha and Omega, the Beginning and the End, the Author and Finisher of *our faith journey*.

> ## REVIVAL TRUTH:
>
> " REVIVAL STARTS when you let go of the ministering and let the Holy Ghost minister in your midst.

So leaders, it's time to *let go of the meeting and ministry* into the capable Hands of the Holy Ghost. To help you with this, there are five things you must do to ensure that you have truly let go. This is your opportunity to receive the Move. I exhort you to:
- Acknowledge the Moving of the Holy Spirit in your midst (this will require that you stop looking at your watch or giving priority to your program).
- Acknowledge that the Fire can burn on specific individuals, who may not be in your leadership team.
- Acknowledge the Revival Leaders in your midst.
- Be willing to be mentored for Revival.
- Learn and adopt the Heart-Posture that hosts the Glory.

THE KEY you are searching for concerning the Move of God is already in your hands. It's you—the one who will decide whether to turn the tap on for Revival... **Revival starts with you—leaders of the Church.**

As soon as you let go of the meeting and allow the Holy Spirit to lead, that's when God will move. Don't hold on to that form of ministry that you think is best for you. God knows that you want to elevate. But true elevation is with the Holy Ghost. Glory-filled Words are about to break upon you as *Mighty Waves*. God is READY to baptise you with the *Dew of His Presence*. It's time to blow the Trumpet and proclaim Heaven's Official Altar Call:

"Now is the Time For Revival"

My Final Exhortation—I Sought for a Man

Here I am Lord. I will be that man. Send me!

In my early days as a new believer, I often listened to this worship song by Ron Kenoly, titled, "If You Can Use Anything Lord, You Can Use Me." With every listen, I could feel the Holy Spirit calling me to a deep place in Him. I didn't yet fully know what it was at that time, but I knew it was *Him*—He was moulding my heart to *know His Will and Desire*. Here's a part of that song:

> "If You can use anything, Lord, You can use me.
> Take my hands, Lord and my feet.
> Touch my heart, Lord, and speak through me.
> If You can use anything Lord, You can use me..."[15]

The Call of God is real—it's life-transforming. A wonderful *opportunity to pursue God's Heart* is before you right now. Will you be a part of His Story? Will you join His Army of Glory Carriers?

PART 12 *The Trumpet Sounds—It's Time for Revival!*

"I sought for a man…"[16] That is God's Revival Call to the Chosen—the Glory Carriers. *The hour of the Holy Spirit's Move has come.* Oh, Burning Ones of the Most High… This is your call to return to that sacred and holy inheritance as *God's Glory Carriers.*

That is my fervent prayer for you. As I come to a close, I pray God will do a deep work in you and call you to *the Deep* in Him. For the Father is in pursuit of a generation hungry for Him, who will worship Him, once again, with all passion and boldness, until His Glory fills their earthen vessels and overflows magnificently, exactly as He intended (John 4:23–24). **May the Glory of His Word fill the Earth.**

Chosen ones, these are more than just passionate words—they are the Father's Heart revealed to us. For God has always wanted to be **in our midst**—it is *His Highest Desire for His people.*

Final reflection:
When thou saidst, "Seek ye My Face; my heart said unto Thee, Thy Face, LORD, will I seek" (Psalm 27:8).

A Declaration Prayer:
Holy Spirit, we are Ready!
Now is the Time!
The Trumpet of Revival Sounds!
The Move of God is Here!
Be it unto us according to Your Word!

In Jesus' name, Amen.

ENDNOTES:
14. Laurie Klein, *I Love You, Lord* (Maranatha! Music, 1978)
15. Jones, Dewitt, and Greg Nelson. Use Me (If You Can Use Anything, Lord, You Can Use Me). Performed by Ron Kenoly. God Is Able, Integrity Music, 1994.
16. Ezekiel 22:30

May **The Light** of the Day of the Lord's Great Awakening **Shine Brightly** Upon You!

About the Author

Norman and his wife, Olivia, are the Senior Pastors of *"The Place Where He Speaks,"* based in Rockhampton, Queensland, Australia. Marked with the Fire of God, Norman began his journey with the Lord in 1999 (in Papua New Guinea).

Keeping true to his *Commissioning Moment with God,* Norman has included this for the benefit of the reader:

> Then Jesus said, "Norman...God Calls you and Anoints you to reach the nations with the Word of God. Preach His Gospel of Peace and Power." Jesus then took three large jars which were filled with Anointing Oil and He poured all the Oil from the jars upon Norman to anoint him as the Carrier, Leader and Servant of The Great Mandate of Revival (the Great Awakening of God)—**Dream— 19 February 2002.**[17] ... Read more in detail of this story and much more in the 'CHOSEN TO CARRY THE GLORY—CARRY THE FIRE OF JESUS' BOOK.

Through many years of nurturing and mentorship under the Holy Spirit, the appointed time has come for the Glory Mandate to be fulfilled and to accomplish the call of mentoring God's people into the Great Revival Fire. For the Glory of the Lord is ready to be manifested to the world, for the shaking of the nations.

ENDNOTE:
17. (Sabadi N.M.T. 2023. Chapter 10 - The Great Induction and Anointing Service, *Chosen to Carry the Glory - Carry the Fire of Jesus,* Norman Sabadi Publishing, Rockhampton, Queensland, Australia pp.165-207).

Other Books by Norman Sabadi

🔥 Wisdom Calls Out To You

🔥 Chosen to Carry the Glory—Carry the Fire of Jesus

Media

Facebook—The Place Where He Speaks Group:
https://www.facebook.com/groups/652589851978873/

YouTube Channel—The Place Where He Speaks
https://www.youtube.com/channel/UCqjypOfptKjmYNVB0_2I2wA

YOUTUBE HANDLE:
@theplacewherehespeaks

Contact Details

We would love to hear from you, about testimonies, praise reports, prayer requests and preaching requests also, or any other thing the Lord has impressed upon you to share. It would be our great honour to receive any communication from you about the *Work of the Great Awakening of God.*

You can reach Pastor Norman through the following methods:

Email: theplacewherehespeaks@gmail.com

Chosen

CHOSEN TO CARRY THE GLORY-CARRY THE FIRE OF JESUS

**YOU CAN SUPPORT
NORMAN SABADI BY:**

* SHARING THE MESSAGE OF THIS BOOK WITH OTHERS.

DONATE TO

PAYPAL:
https://www.paypal.com/paypalme/normsabadi

Thank you so much for your support and may the Lord bless you abundantly

www.ingramcontent.com/pod-product-compliance
Lightning Source LLC
Chambersburg PA
CBHW070724160426
43192CB00009B/1304